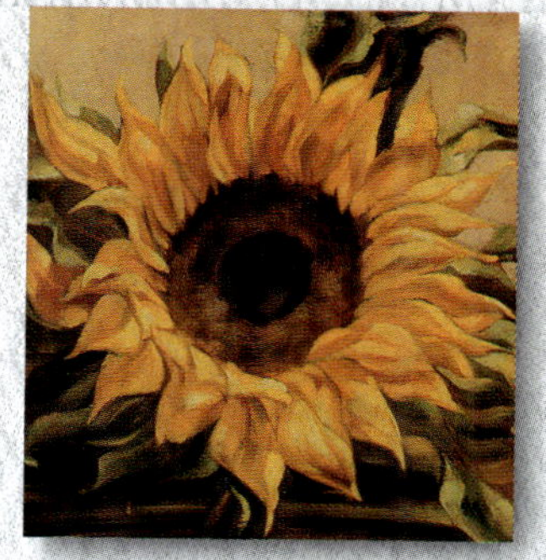

Still Lifes

One of the most wonderful things about painting still lifes is that you have complete control over the arrangement—what objects to include, where to place them, and how to light them. And there is no better way to render the many textures and varied forms of a still life than with oil paint. The variety of effects you can achieve with oil is virtually limitless, and its slow drying time allows you to take your time perfecting the forms and making changes. In this book, you'll find 12 step-by-step lessons from 3 renowned oil painting artists. Individually they'll introduce you to their own perspectives on tools, techniques, and methods for painting still lifes. With every engaging lesson, you'll discover the information and inspiration you need to choose your own subjects, develop your own style, and paint your own captivating still lifes in oil!

CONTENTS

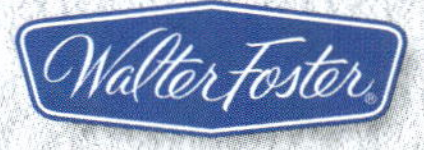

Choosing Your Materials

When you visit the art supply store, it's easy to get carried away by the exciting array of choices on display. Though you may be tempted to bring home one of everything, you'll need only a few select tools and materials to start painting. You can begin with a minimal investment, but it's wise to choose the best supplies that you can afford. Not only will high-quality materials themselves last longer, they'll also contribute to finished paintings that can endure for generations! On these pages you'll find basic descriptions of the essential tools you'll need to begin painting; to learn more, refer to *Oil Painting Materials and Their Uses* by William F. Powell in Walter Foster's Artist's Library series.

BUYING OIL PAINTS

Oil paints are available in several different grades, including students' grade and artists' grade. Artists' grade paints are a little more expensive, but they contain better-quality pigment and fewer additives, making more intense colors that stay true longer.

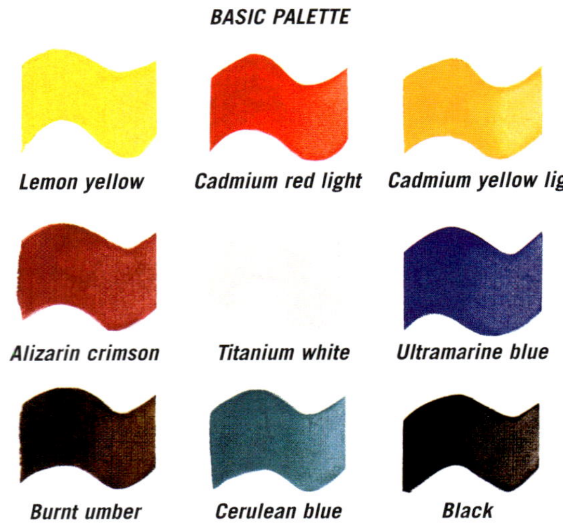

PICKING A PALETTE OF COLORS

The nine colors shown above are a good basic palette (with a warm and cool version of each of the primary colors). Each artist featured in this book has some unique colors in his or her palette, so these lessons will give you an opportunity to try other colors as well. There are many ways to mix colors—and the more you practice and experiment, the easier it will seem! For more information about color theory and mixing colors, refer to *Color* by William F. Powell in Walter Foster's How to Draw and Paint series.

Adding to the Palette

For the lessons in this book, you'll need to add one or more of the colors listed below to your basic palette. (Refer to each project for a complete listing of colors needed.)

- ❑ brilliant green light
- ❑ brilliant yellow
- ❑ burnt sienna
- ❑ cadmium orange
- ❑ cad. orange light
- ❑ cad. orange med.
- ❑ cad. yellow med.
- ❑ dioxazine purple
- ❑ flesh
- ❑ Indian red
- ❑ Indian yellow
- ❑ light blue-violet
- ❑ magenta
- ❑ Naples yellow
- ❑ olive green
- ❑ Payne's gray
- ❑ permanent green
- ❑ perm. green light
- ❑ permanent rose
- ❑ phthalo blue
- ❑ phthalo green
- ❑ phthalo violet
- ❑ Prussian blue
- ❑ purple madder
- ❑ raw sienna
- ❑ red ochre
- ❑ sap green
- ❑ transparent orange
- ❑ yellow-green
- ❑ yellow ochre
- ❑ zinc white
- ❑ med. magenta acrylic paint

WORKING WITH SUPPORTS

The surface on which you paint (generally canvas or wood) is called the *support.* You can stretch canvas yourself, but it's simpler to purchase prestretched, preprimed canvas (stapled to a frame) or canvas board (canvas glued to cardboard). If you work on wood or any other porous material, you must apply a primer first to seal the surface so the oil paints will adhere to the support (instead of soaking through).

FINDING THE RIGHT SIZE Stretched canvases, canvas boards, and wood boards are available in standard sizes. If you want a custom size, you can stretch your own canvas or cut down a wood board.

CHOOSING AND CARING FOR BRUSHES

Oil painting brushes vary greatly in size, shape, and texture. There is no universal standard for brush sizes, so they vary slightly among manufacturers. Some brushes are sized by number, and others are sized by inches or fractions of inches. Just get the brushes that are appropriate for the size of your paintings and are comfortable for you to work with. The six brushes pictured below are a good starting set; you can always add to your collection later. Brushes are also categorized by the material of their bristles; natural-hair brushes are best for oil painting. Cleaning and caring for your brushes is essential—always rinse them out well with turpentine and store them bristle-side up or flat (never bristle-side down).

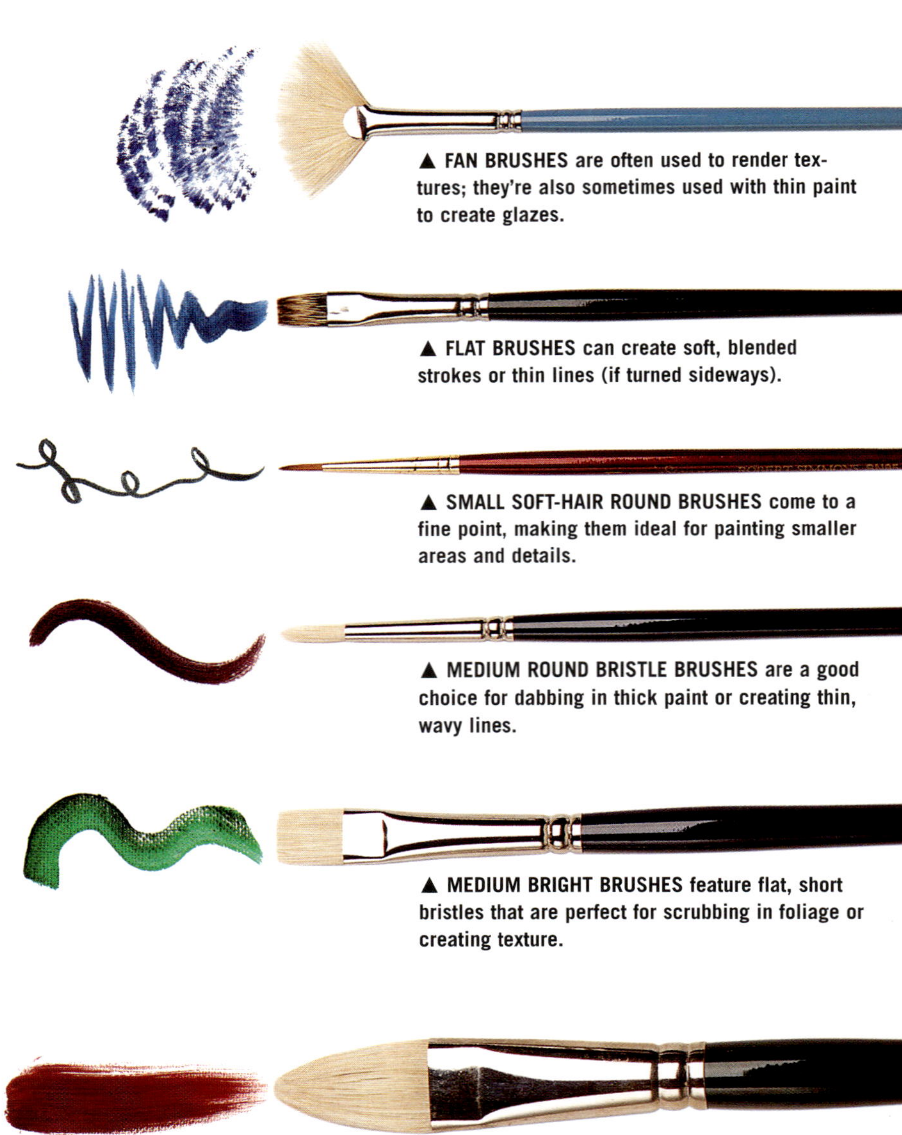

▲ **FAN BRUSHES** are often used to render textures; they're also sometimes used with thin paint to create glazes.

▲ **FLAT BRUSHES** can create soft, blended strokes or thin lines (if turned sideways).

▲ **SMALL SOFT-HAIR ROUND BRUSHES** come to a fine point, making them ideal for painting smaller areas and details.

▲ **MEDIUM ROUND BRISTLE BRUSHES** are a good choice for dabbing in thick paint or creating thin, wavy lines.

▲ **MEDIUM BRIGHT BRUSHES** feature flat, short bristles that are perfect for scrubbing in foliage or creating texture.

▲ **BRISTLE-HAIR FILBERTS** can hold a considerable amount of paint, and they are generally used for blocking in or painting large areas.

UNDERSTANDING ADDITIVES

Oil painting mediums modify the consistency of your paint, and there are many different types available at art supply stores. Some (such as linseed oil) thin out the paint and others (such as copal) speed drying time. Still others alter the finish or texture of the paint. From the many choices available, you'll want to select some type of oil medium to moisten the paint when it gets dry or stiff and to thin it for glazing and underpaintings. Turpentine or mineral spirits can be used for initial washes or underpainting—or even to clean your brushes—but you won't want to use them as a replacement for medium. Although some artists do like to use turpentine as a thinner (mixing a small quantity with their oil paints), other oil mediums have the advantage of actually helping preserve the paint.

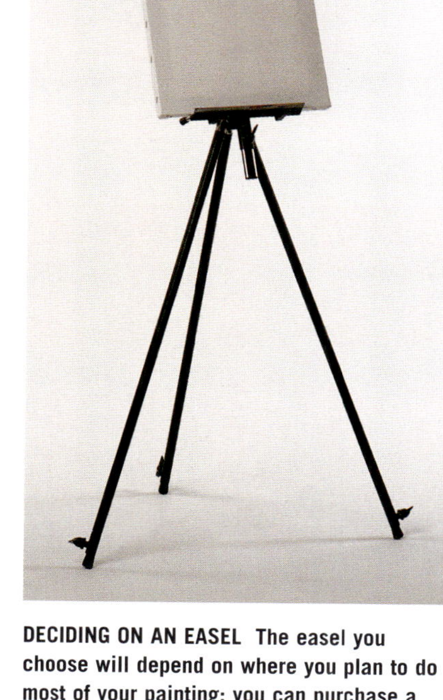

DECIDING ON AN EASEL The easel you choose will depend on where you plan to do most of your painting; you can purchase a studio or tabletop easel for painting indoors or a portable easel for painting outdoors.

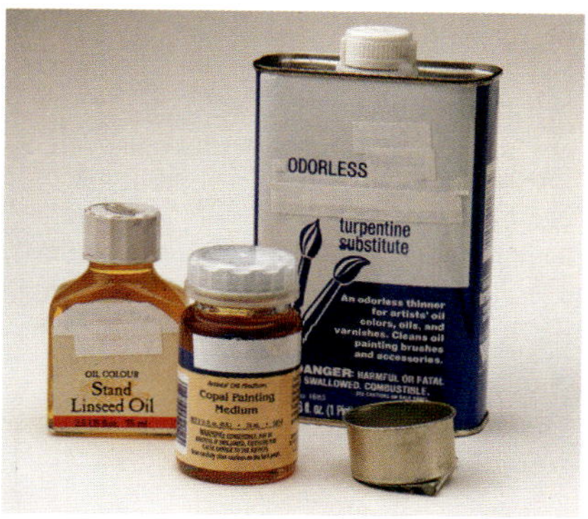

USING MEDIUMS In addition to the medium you select, be sure to purchase a glass or metal cup to hold the medium. Some containers have a clip built into the bottom that attaches easily to your mixing palette.

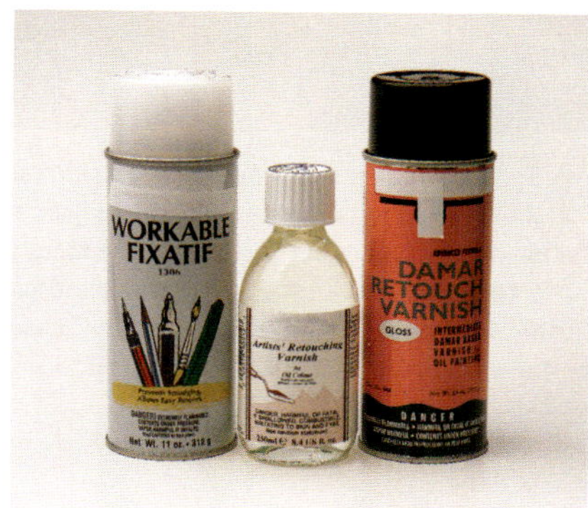

FINISHING UP Varnishes are used to protect your painting—spray-on varnishes temporarily set the paint, and brush-on varnishes permanently protect your work. See the manufacturer's instructions for application guidelines.

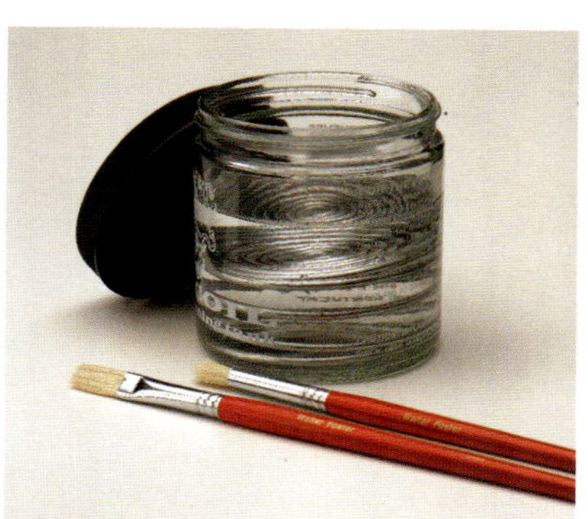

CLEANING BRUSHES Purchasing a jar that contains a screen or coil can save some time and mess. As you rub the brush against the coil, it loosens the paint from the bristles and separates the sediment from the solvent. Once the paint has been removed, you can use brush soap and warm (never hot) water to remove any residual paint. Then reshape the bristles of the brush with your fingers, and lay it out to dry.

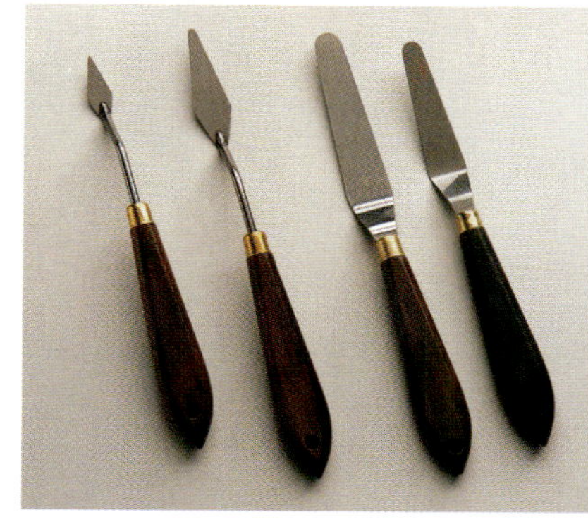

UTILIZING PAINTING AND PALETTE KNIVES Painting knives generally have a small, diamond-shaped head, which is used to apply paint, whereas palette knives (also called "mixing knives") usually have a longer, more rectangular blade. Palette knives can be used either to mix paint on your palette or to apply paint to your support. Some knives have raised handles, which help you avoid getting wet paint on your hand as you work.

CHECKLIST OF BASICS

Below is a list of the materials you'll need to purchase to get started painting in oils. (For specifics, refer to the suggested brushes and colors on page 2.)

- ❑ 9 basic oil colors
- ❑ 6 brushes
- ❑ Medium (copal or linseed oil)
- ❑ Thinner (mineral spirits or turpentine)
- ❑ Palette and palette paper
- ❑ Containers for thinner and medium
- ❑ Palette knife
- ❑ Easel
- ❑ Supports
- ❑ Paper towels

SELECTING A PALETTE

Whatever type of mixing palette you choose—glass, wood, plastic, or paper—make sure it's easy to clean and large enough for mixing your colors. Glass is a great surface for mixing paints and is very durable. Palette paper is disposable, so cleanup is simple, and you can always purchase an airtight plastic box (or paint seal) to keep your leftover paint fresh between painting sessions.

GATHERING THE EXTRAS

Paper towels or lint-free rags are invaluable when oil painting; you can use them to clean your tools and brushes, and you can also use them as painting tools to scrub in washes or soften edges. Some type of paint box is also useful for holding all your materials. In addition, you may want charcoal or a pencil for sketching and a mahlstick to help you steady your hand when working on a large support.

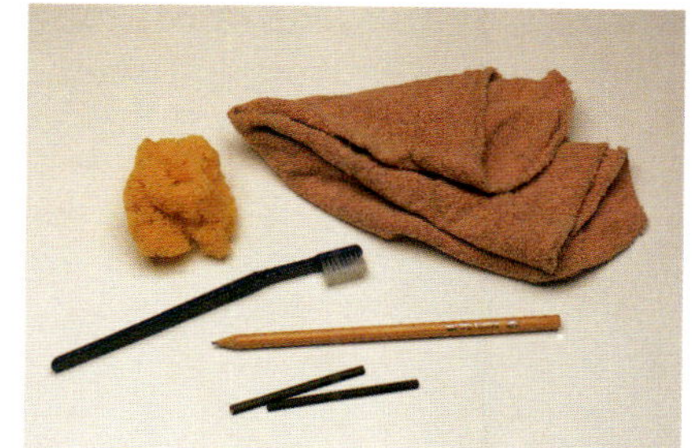

CONSIDERING EXTRAS In addition to the basic tools, you may also want to acquire a silk sea sponge and an old toothbrush to render special effects. Even though you may not use these additional items for every oil painting you work on, it's a good idea to keep them on hand in case you need them.

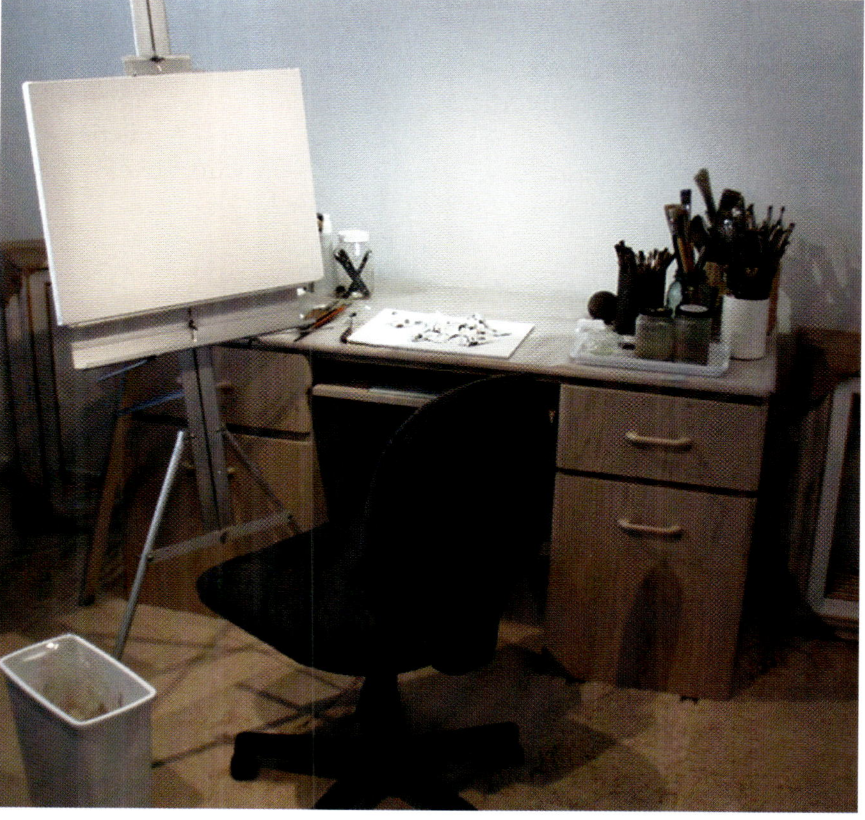

SETTING UP YOUR WORK SPACE How you set up your work station will depend on whether you are right- or left-handed. Try to keep your supplies in the same place, so that each time you sit down to paint, you don't have to waste time searching for anything. If natural light is unavailable, make sure you have sufficient artificial lighting, and above all else, make sure you're comfortable!

Setting Up a Still Life

by Tom Swimm

Still life paintings traditionally depict a number of inanimate objects, such as fruit, vegetables, glassware, pottery, and other household items—elements that can be arranged in a variety of different ways. But there are a few basic rules you should keep in mind when setting up any still-life composition. First a good composition groups the elements into a cohesive, harmonious unit, and it directs the viewer's eye around the painting with its use of interesting shapes, colors, curving lines, and diagonals. And an effective visual path always leads toward a distinct center of interest, or *focal point*. In addition, the focal point is usually placed off center, which creates more visual interest than placing it directly in the middle of the painting. Another way to build a good composition is by overlapping some objects to create a sense of depth. Here Tom Swimm paints a simple but dynamic scene using all the basic rules. He arranges objects of varying shapes and textures for interest, overlaps some of them for depth, and places the focal point—the wine bottle and glass—slightly off center. And the visual path he creates with the elements of his scene draws the viewer's eye into the painting and along the line of fruit and cheese, heading toward the focal point.

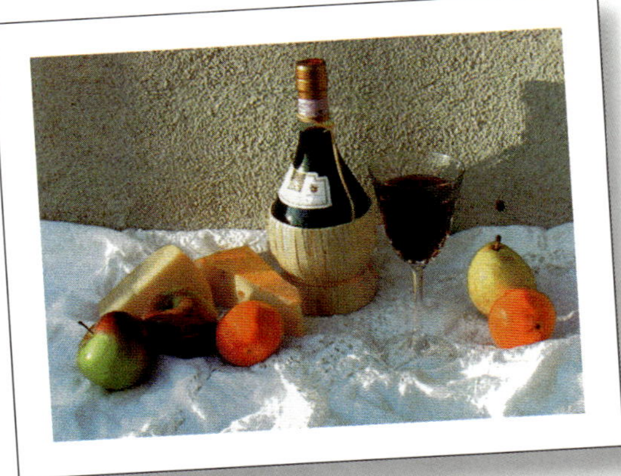

◄ **ARRANGING THE OBJECTS** For this painting, I wanted a classic "old world" composition, so I selected several items that have a classic appeal. Then I photographed several different arrangements until I found one I liked. (See page 8 for more on working from photos.)

Color Palette

alizarin crimson, burnt sienna, cadmium orange light, cadmium red light, cadmium yellow light, cerulean blue, Indian red, light blue-violet, medium magenta (acrylic), Naples yellow, Payne's gray, permanent green light, phthalo violet, raw sienna, sap green, titanium white, yellow ochre

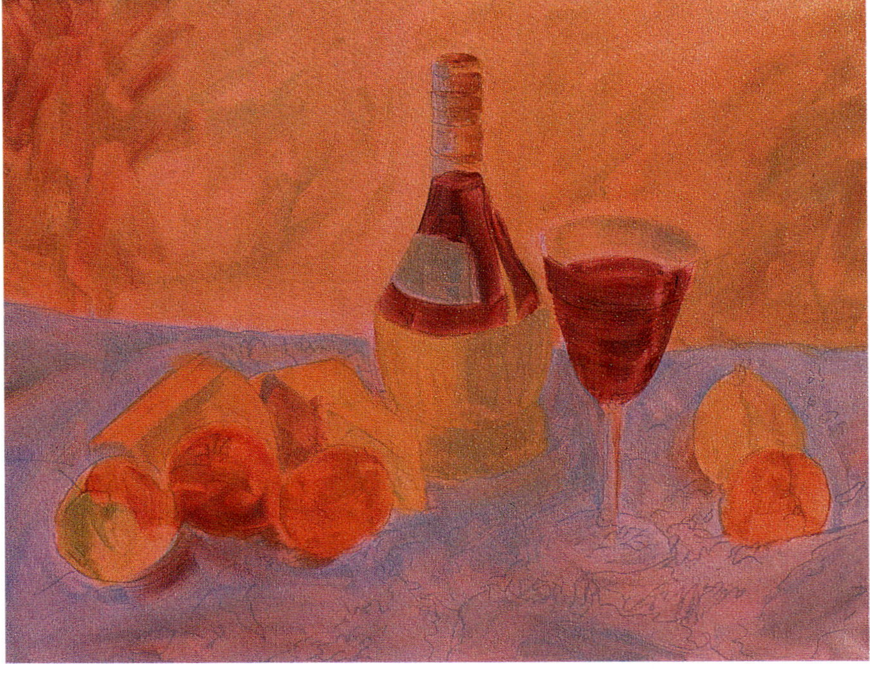

1 To begin, I sketch the basic composition with a fine-point marker. Then I cover the entire canvas with a thin base coat of magenta acrylic paint to create an overall warm tone. Next I create a rough guide for my painting by blocking in the basic colors and values with thin washes. I use cerulean blue for the tablecloth and some of the shaded areas, and I use alizarin crimson for the wine bottle and glass. I define the cheese, the fruit, the background, and the bottom half of the wine bottle with burnt sienna, yellow ochre, and sap green.

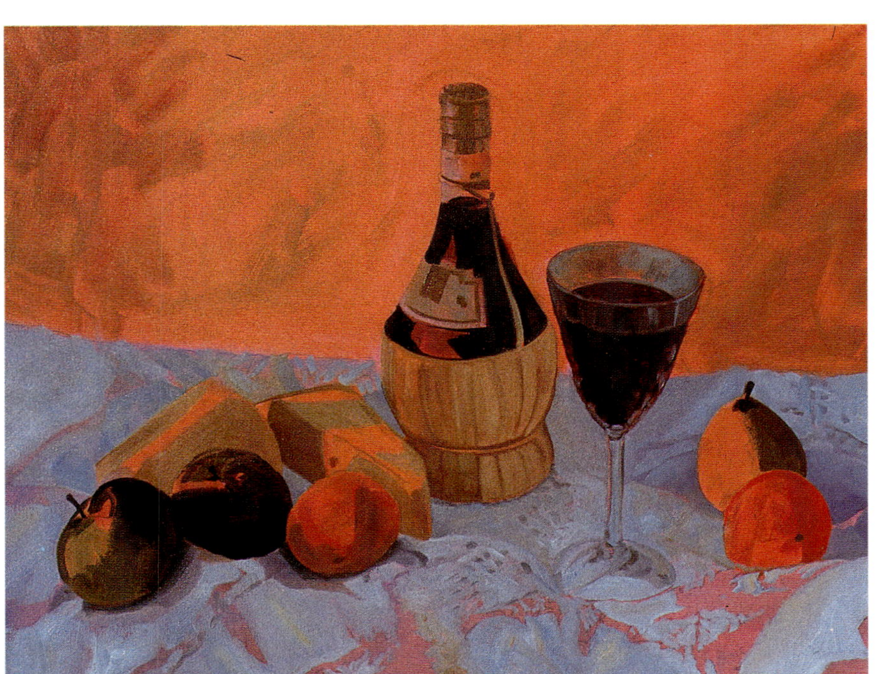

2 Now I use a medium flat brush to pick up various mixes of alizarin crimson and Payne's gray, which I use to paint the wine and the darkest shadows on the fruit. Then I mix raw sienna and sap green for the cheese, apples, and other details in the wine bottle, adding alizarin crimson and yellow ochre for the oranges. I also define the shadows of the tablecloth, first using cerulean blue and light blue-violet for the darkest areas, and then adding titanium white for some of the highlights. I use this same color mixture to paint the wine glass. Then, in the shadow areas of the cloth that are warmed by the reflected light from the bottle and glass, I paint a little of the raw sienna and sap green mixture.

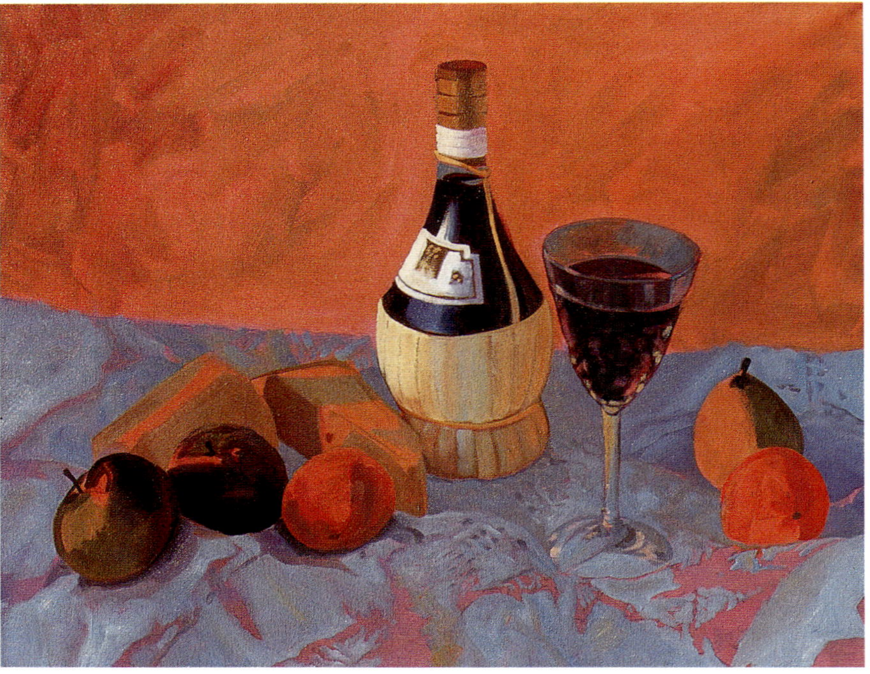

3 Next I add the mid-range values of color and the highlights to the wine bottle and glass. The foil around the upper neck of the bottle is a mixture of raw sienna, Payne's gray, and yellow ochre. Using a medium flat brush, I blend the highlights and shadows to create shape and volume. Then I mix lighter variations of these colors with titanium white and light blue-violet for the bottom half of the wine bottle. I also use these colors for the highlights on the wine glass and the top of the bottle. I paint the shadows on the labels with a mix of phthalo violet, light blue-violet, and titanium white, and I use Naples yellow and titanium white for the brightest highlights on the left side.

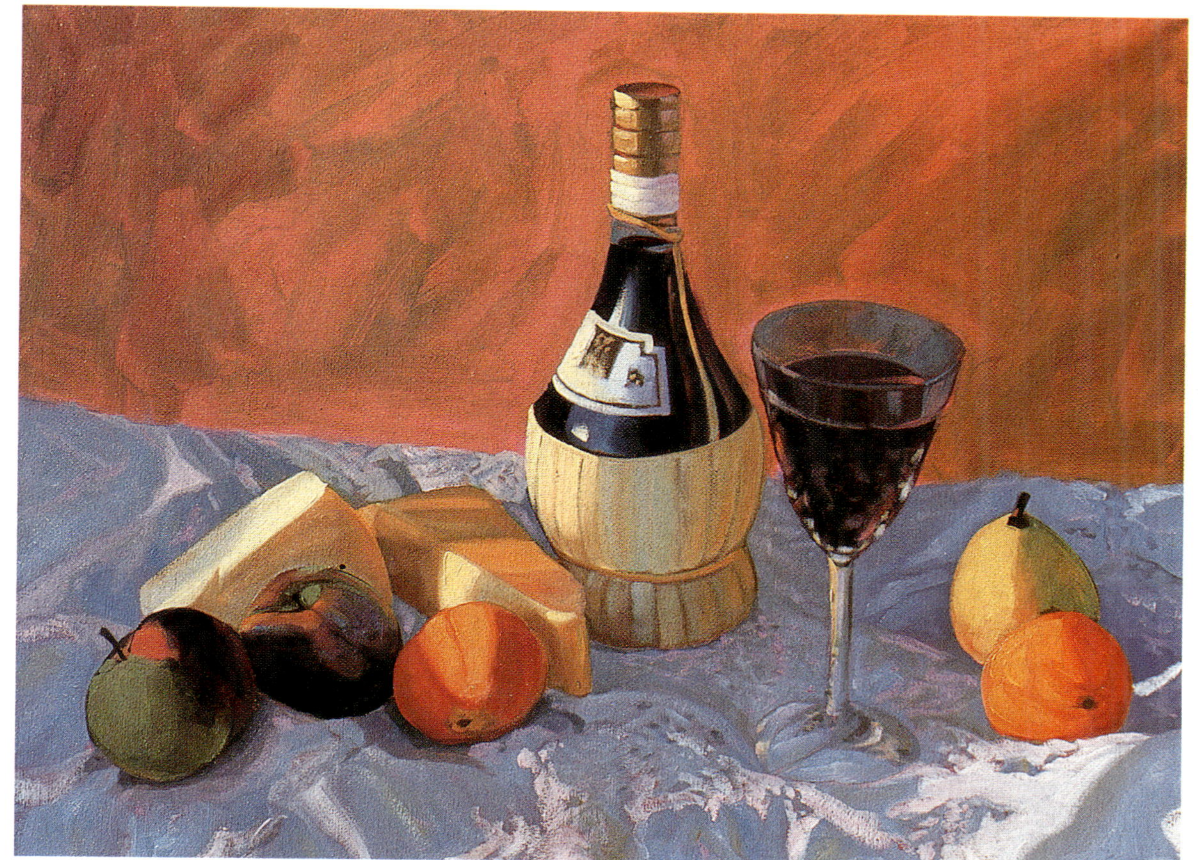

  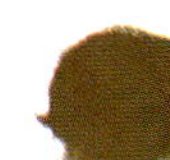  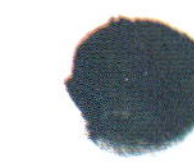

DARK VALUES (LEFT TO RIGHT):
Alizarin crimson + Payne's gray
Cerulean blue + sap green + phthalo violet
Raw sienna + sap green
Light blue-violet + titanium white
Cerulean blue + light blue-violet

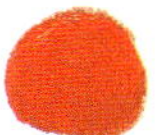 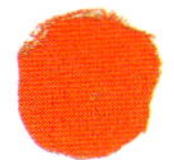 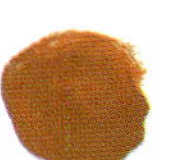  

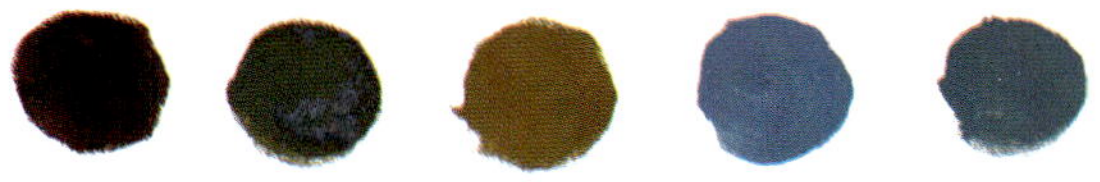

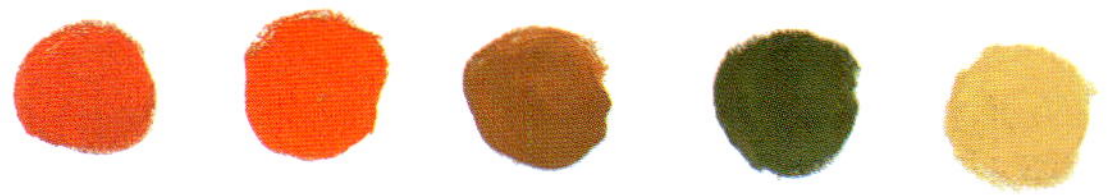

MID-RANGE VALUES (LEFT TO RIGHT):
Cadmium red light + cadmium orange light + titanium white
Cadmium orange light + titanium white
Raw sienna + cadmium orange light
Sap green + yellow ochre
Naples yellow + titanium white

4 Now I develop the wine, cheese, cloth, and shadow colors (see color samples above), defining the details and areas that are separated by light and shadow. I add Payne's gray to darken the values and titanium white to brighten the colors and highlights. I keep my brushstrokes varied, using a thicker mixture for texture and blending the transition areas with the flat side of the brush. Then I mix phthalo violet, light blue-violet, and titanium white for the areas of the tablecloth that receive the most light.

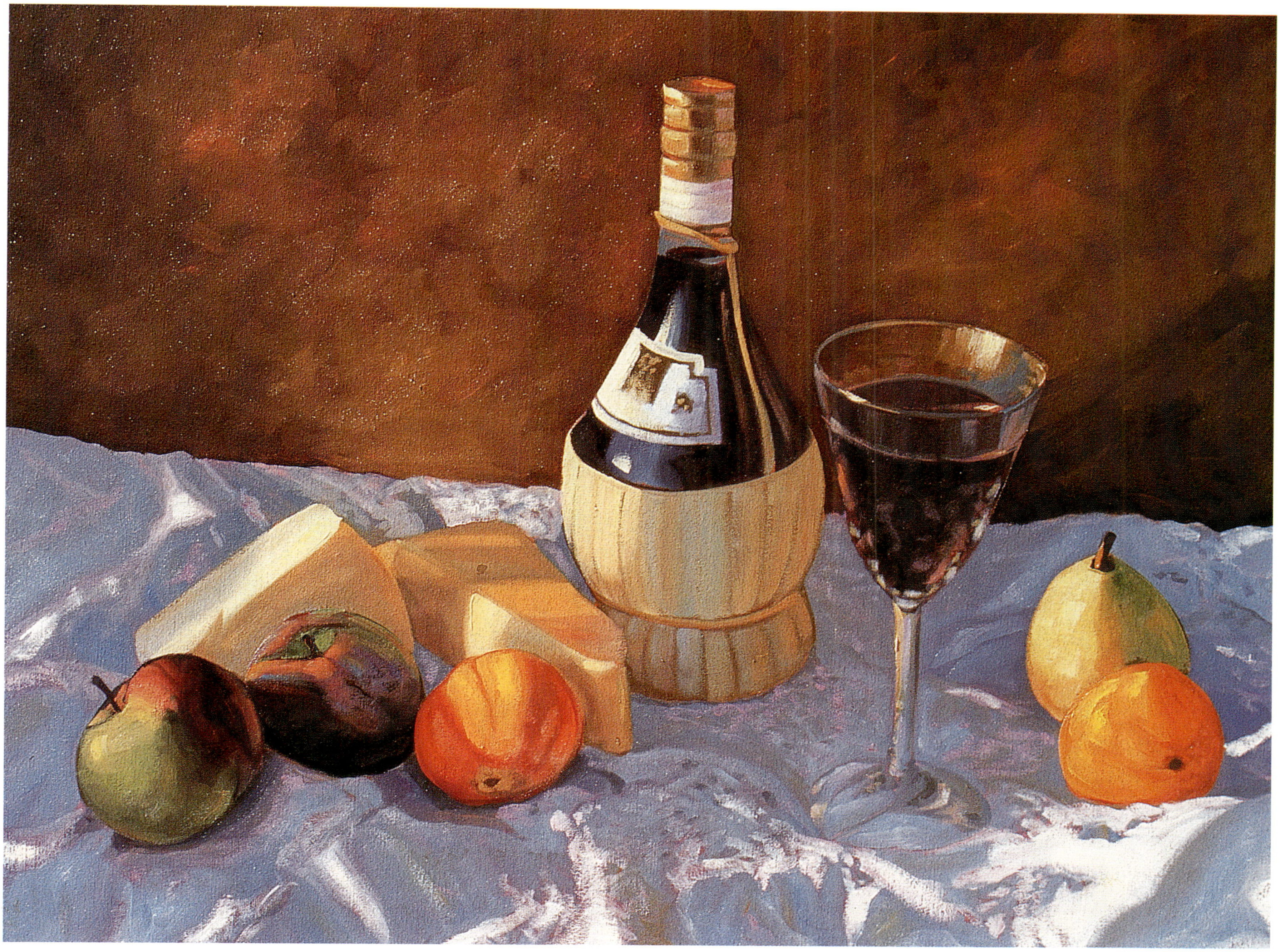

5 I decide to alter the background to add more contrast and drama. I mix burnt sienna, yellow ochre, Payne's gray, and Indian red, applying these colors in loose, random brushstrokes and being careful not to overwork any specific area. To finish the painting, I add a few bright accents to the lightest areas of the composition using mixes of titanium white, cadmium yellow light, permanent green light, and cadmium orange light. After that, I pour myself a glass of wine and toast my newest creation!

"Finding" Compositions

by Tom Swimm

Sometimes the objects of a still life are selected and carefully arranged by the artist, but other times interesting combinations of shapes, textures, and colors are "found" in the everyday world. Whether you deliberately arrange the elements yourself or find a ready-made composition by chance, your setup should always convey a visual theme, focusing on the subject that is your inspiration. Artist Tom Swimm is often drawn to nautical themes, particularly the shape and color of maritime "tools of the trade." He was instantly captivated by this harbor boat scene composed of colorful ropes and the fascinating shadows they cast on the deck. Not everyone has access to a boat harbor like the one where Tom made his nautical find, but there are plenty of other places to look for inspiration. Try taking a walk around a park or through a residential neighborhood; you may be surprised by the compositions you find.

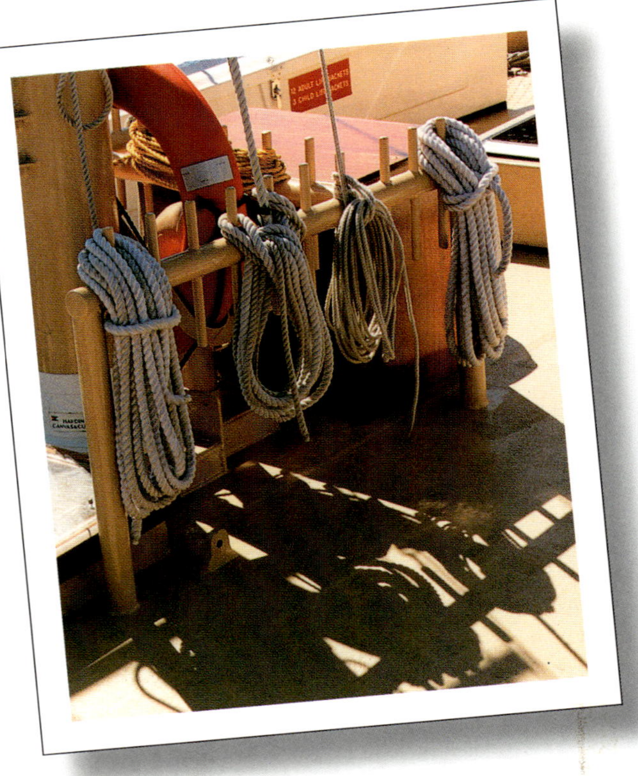

► **PHOTOGRAPHING THE SCENE** The shape and color of nautical objects make for wonderful still-life compositions. As I walked around the deck of this boat, I took numerous photos at various angles; I wanted to give myself a lot of choices for the final composition. But I kept coming back to this spot—the reflected light created an interesting contrast with the cast shadows and seemed to tell a story. I decided to crop the photo to make the ropes the dominant visual element, allowing the shadows to fill in the lower half of the image.

Color Palette

Alizarin crimson, brilliant yellow, burnt sienna, cadmium orange light, cadmium red light, cadmium yellow light, cerulean blue, flesh, Indian red, light blue-violet, magenta (acrylic), Payne's gray, phthalo blue, phthalo violet, Prussian blue, raw sienna, sap green, titanium white, yellow ochre

MID-RANGE VALUES

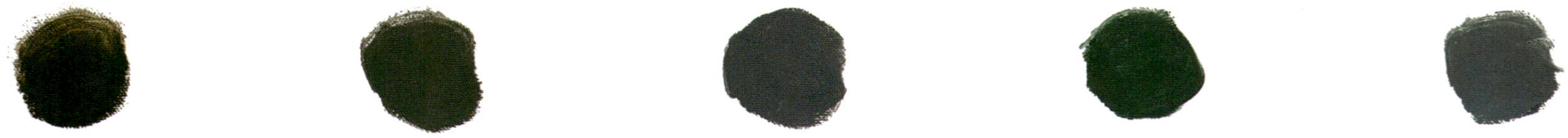

Payne's gray + cerulean blue + flesh + Indian red

Payne's gray + cerulean blue + phthalo violet

Payne's gray + cerulean blue + phthalo violet + titanium white

Cerulean blue + flesh

Cerulean blue + flesh + titanium white

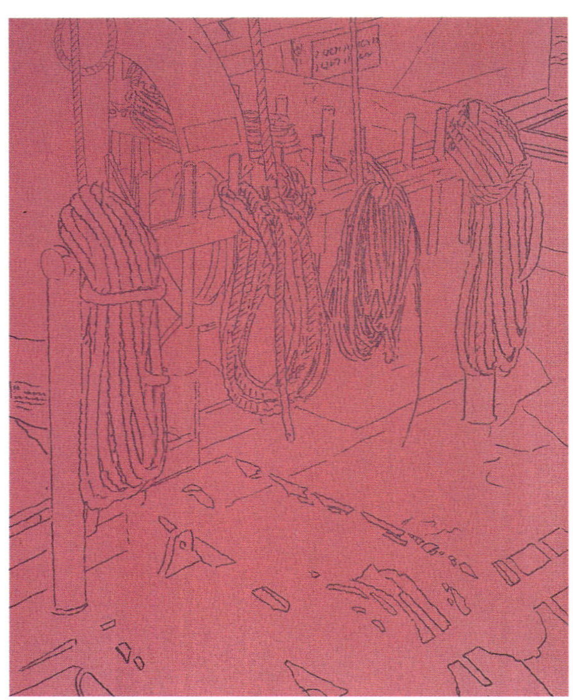

1 First I project the photo image onto a canvas and use a fine-point marker to sketch the composition. Then I cover the canvas with a thin wash of medium magenta acrylic paint. I begin all my paintings with this technique because the base color warms the colors that will be applied over it and adds luminosity to the highlights. You can experiment with different underpainting colors; try blues and greens to give the finished painting a cooler hue or reds and yellows for a warmer result.

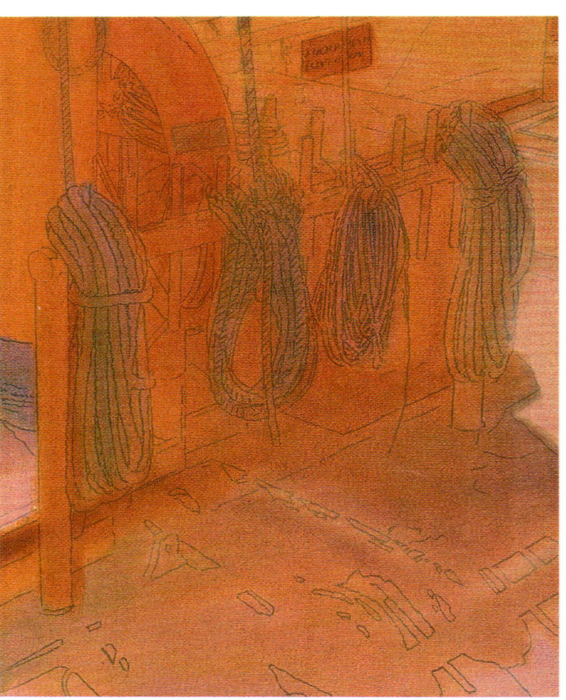

2 I establish the basic values with thinned color mixtures, applying the paint loosely with a large flat brush. I use flesh for the lightest areas and yellow ochre for the highlights at the upper right. Then I block in the mast, the life preserver, and the wooden posts with burnt sienna. For the ropes and the shadows in the foreground, I add Payne's gray. Detail isn't important at this stage; this layer is a rough guide, so it's okay to paint "outside the lines."

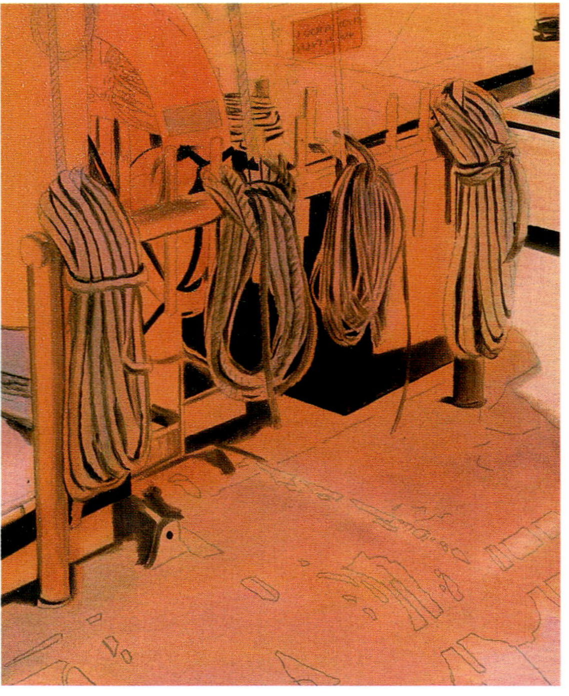

3 Now I begin layering lighter colors on top of the underpainting to create a sense of depth and texture. First I want to establish the darkest colors, defining the deep shadows. Using a medium flat brush, I draw the outlines of the ropes and paint the shadowed areas. Instead of using black from the tube, I mix equal parts of alizarin crimson, sap green, and Prussian blue to create a rich, deep hue (adding even more alizarin crimson to this mix for warmer values).

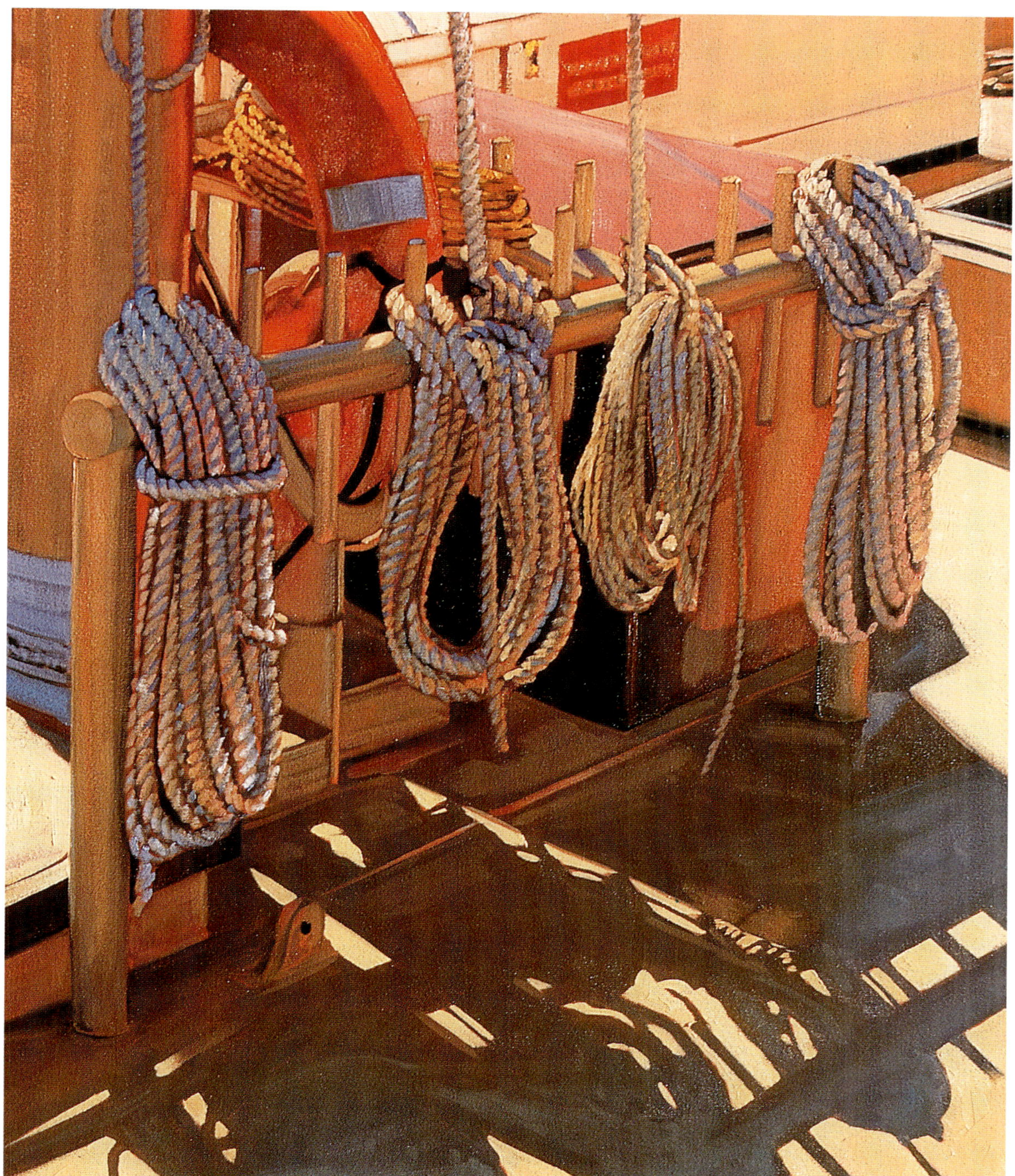

6 I apply highlights of flesh, cadmium yellow light, and titanium white to the top of the railing, the posts, and the ropes in direct sunlight. For the deck, I first apply a mix of brilliant yellow and titanium white. Then I paint over it with an even lighter color—a mix of cadmium yellow light, cadmium orange light, and titanium white. I paint the remaining highlights in the life preserver with cadmium yellow light and cadmium red light, and I blend flesh into this mixture for a few accents in the ropes and shadows. Finally I step back to look at my painting and make a few minor refinements to harmonize the color and details.

ROPES

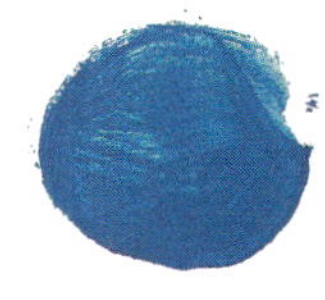

Phthalo blue + light blue violet

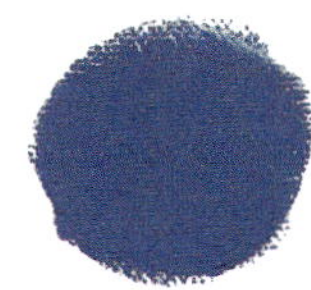

Light blue violet + titanium white

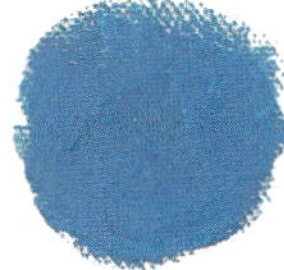

Phthalo blue + light blue violet + titanium white

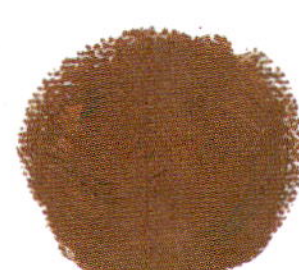

Phthalo violet + flesh + titanium white

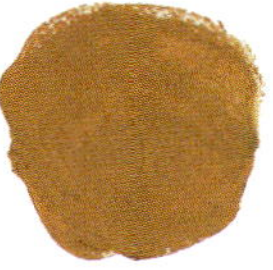

Raw sienna + titanium white

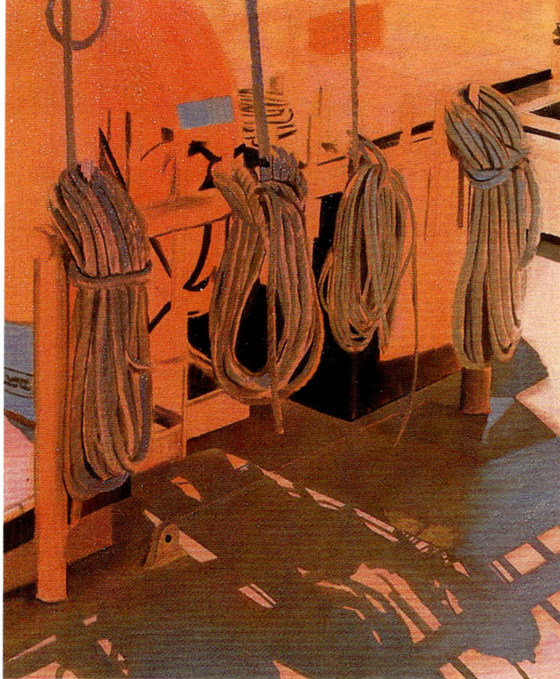

4 Next I use a medium flat brush to blend in the mid-range values. For the foreground shadows, I add subtle variations of Payne's gray, cerulean blue, flesh, Indian red, phthalo violet, and titanium white (see color samples on page 6). The shadows closest to the ropes reflect the warm colors of the wood and gradually become bluer in the foreground. For harmony, I use the same colors to build up the shape and detail in the ropes, the metal plate on the mast, and the label on the life preserver.

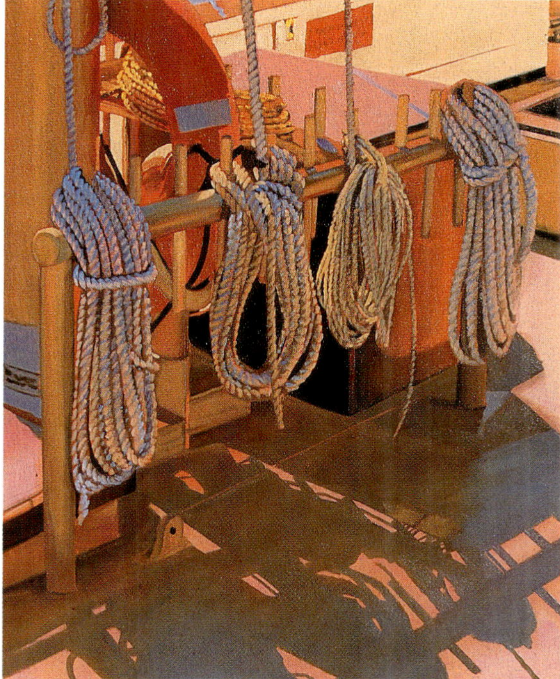

5 Now I paint the ropes, applying the blues first and then adding warmer colors in between for depth (see color samples above right). Next I add highlights in the mast and wooden post with yellow ochre mixed with cerulean blue. For the dark wood and the life preserver, I use Indian red and burnt sienna, and I highlight the ropes with a mix of cadmium yellow light and cadmium orange light. Then I paint the bright background areas using cadmium red light mixed with white and brilliant yellow mixed with white.

HIGHLIGHTS

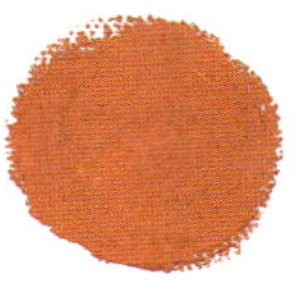

Cadmium red light + flesh + white

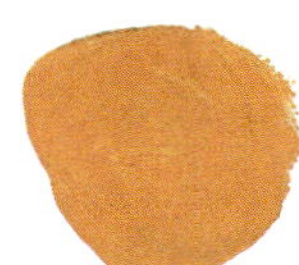

Flesh + yellow ochre + titanium white

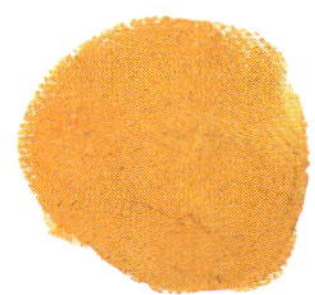

Brilliant yellow + titanium white

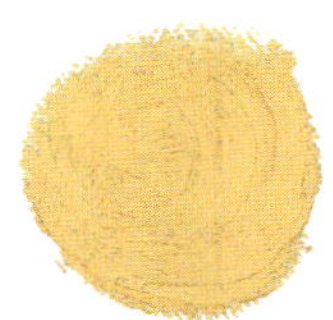

Cadmium orange light + cadmium yellow light + titanium white

Working from Photos

by Tom Swimm

Although painting a still-life composition from an actual setup can be a wonderful experience, there are times when using a photo reference can be a plus—or even a necessity. One reason to use photos is to capture a fleeting moment in time, such as quickly shifting light or a fast-wilting flower. Another reason for taking photographs is to allow yourself the luxury of experimenting with different setups in order to find the best one—and then you have a permanent record of it for reference. Rather than drawing several thumbnail sketches, it's easier and more practical to compare the photos side by side so you can decide which is the most successful arrangement. Then you can paint directly from the photo, instead of re-creating the setup you have chosen. For this painting, artist Tom Swimm took several photographs of the paint tubes in haphazard arrangements until he found the most pleasing composition. Without the photo, he would have had a difficult time reconstructing the random arrangement. And, in this case, Tom had another reason to use a photograph: He needed to use the tubes of oil for the painting!

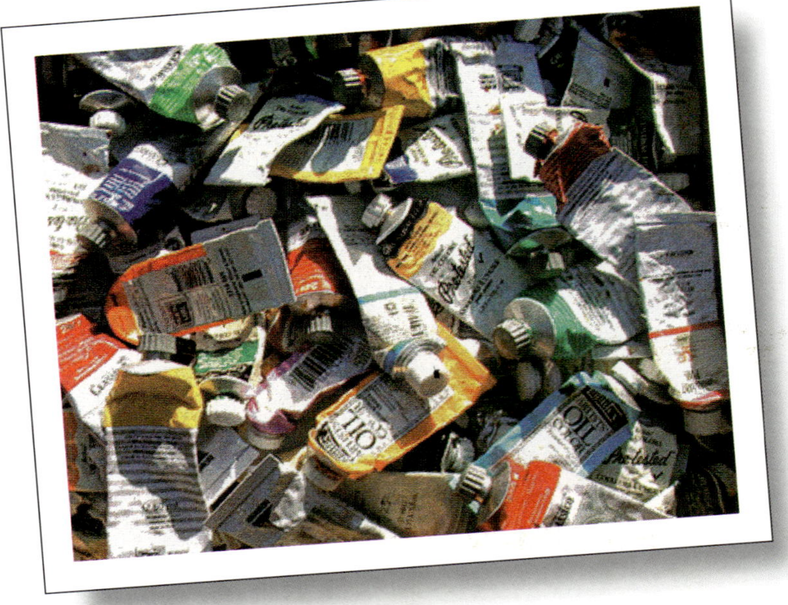

PREPARING THE SUBJECT I didn't spend a lot of time arranging the elements. I just photographed the paint box from above, shook it up a few times to change the arrangement, and then photographed it again from different viewpoints.

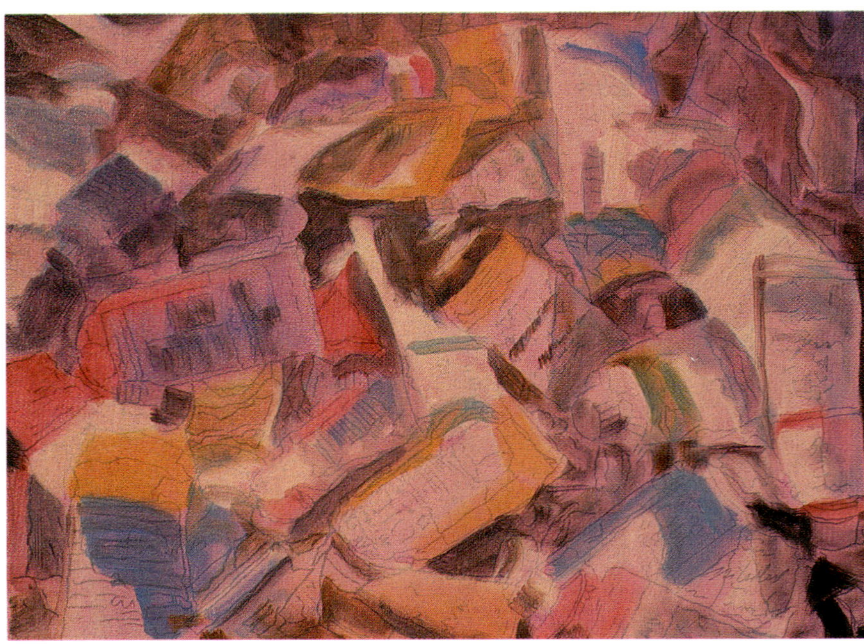

1 First I use a fine-point marker to draw a rough outline on my support. Then I cover the canvas with a thin base of medium magenta acrylic. Next I define the basic shapes and color values, using a large flat brush and thin, wet washes of flesh, alizarin crimson, cerulean blue, sap green, and Payne's gray. At this stage, I'm most interested in establishing the basic colors, so I paint thinly enough to let the drawing show through.

2 I start by defining the darkest colors and values with a combination of Payne's gray and cerulean blue. I fill in the shadow areas while the base coat is still wet, working the paint into the colors already established for variation and texture. With a medium flat brush, I define the label and lettering details and intensify the shadows with a "black" mixture of alizarin crimson, sap green, and Prussian blue (adding more alizarin crimson for warmer hues.

Color Palette

alizarin crimson, brilliant green light, burnt sienna, cadmium orange light, cadmium red light, cadmium yellow light, cerulean blue, flesh, light blue-violet, medium magenta (acrylic), Payne's gray, phthalo violet, Prussian blue, raw sienna, sap green, titanium white

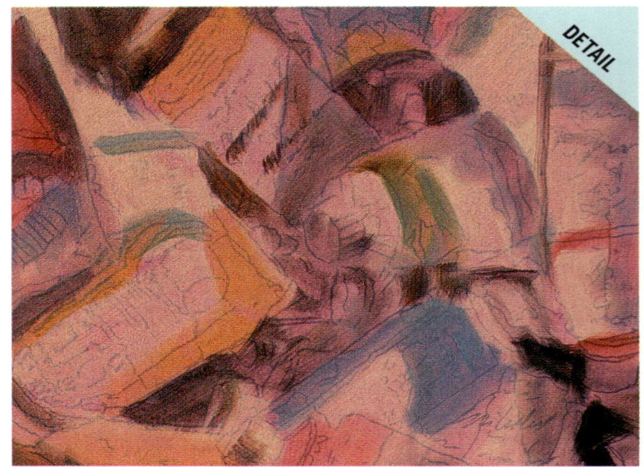

WORKING THIN TO THICK Here I'm using a a technique known as "fat over lean." My first applications are thin enough for my initial sketch to show through, but as I progress, I gradually thicken the paint.

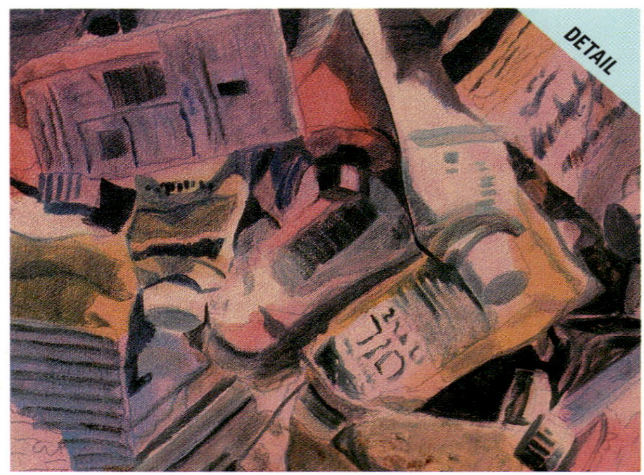

WORKING DARK TO LIGHT I break my subject down visually into three categories: dark values, middle values, and highlights. Then I establish these values in layers, painting from dark to light.

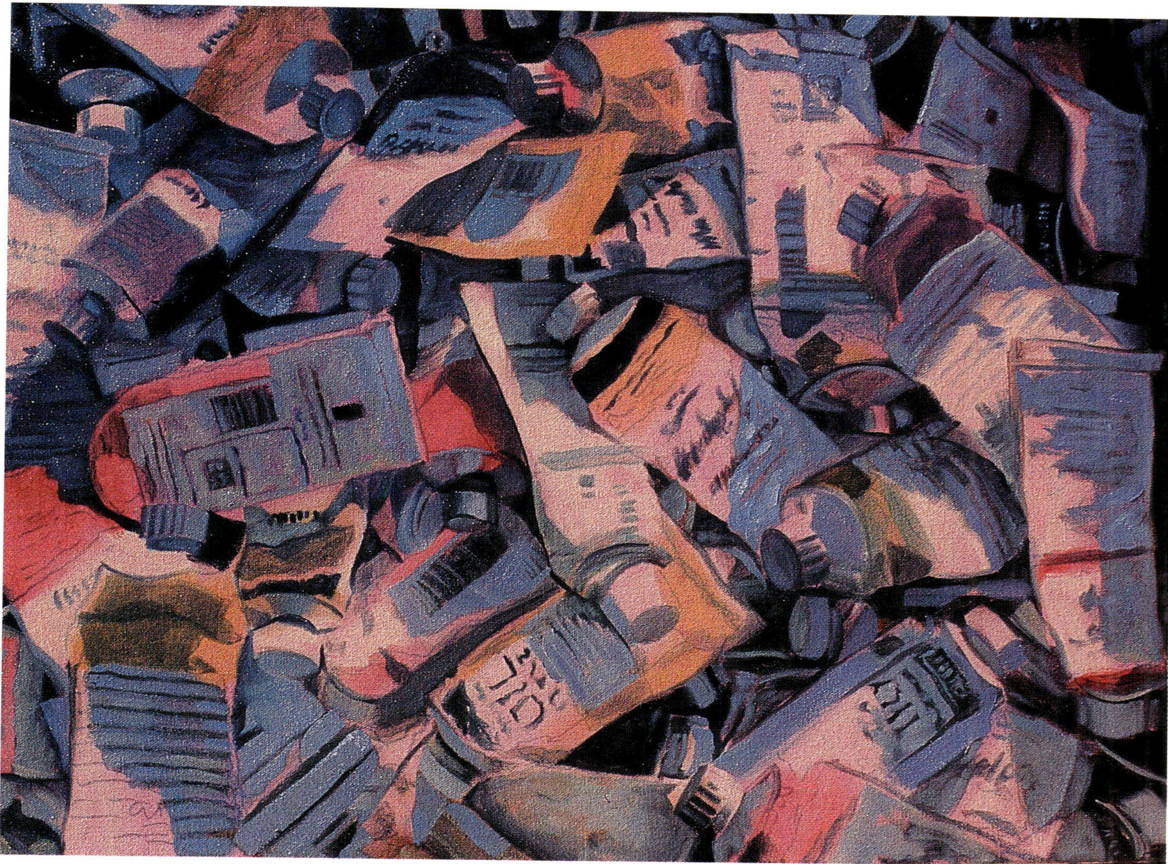

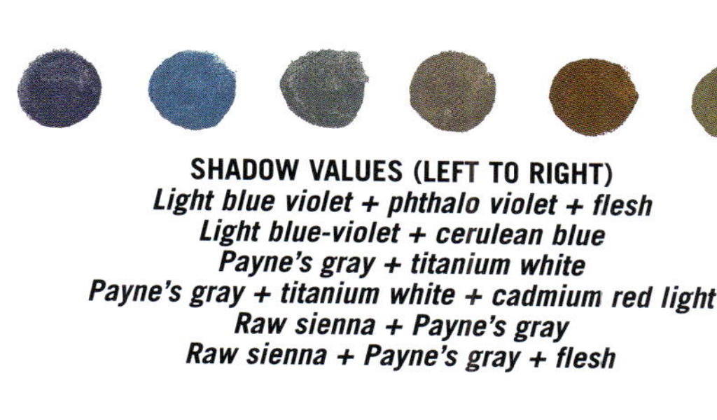

SHADOW VALUES (LEFT TO RIGHT)
Light blue violet + phthalo violet + flesh
Light blue-violet + cerulean blue
Payne's gray + titanium white
Payne's gray + titanium white + cadmium red light
Raw sienna + Payne's gray
Raw sienna + Payne's gray + flesh

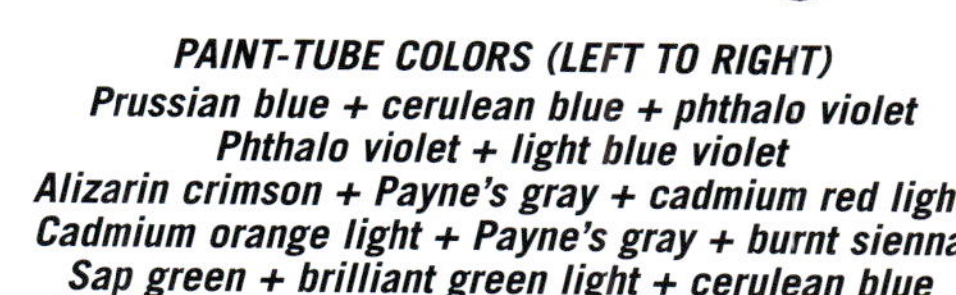

PAINT-TUBE COLORS (LEFT TO RIGHT)
Prussian blue + cerulean blue + phthalo violet
Phthalo violet + light blue violet
Alizarin crimson + Payne's gray + cadmium red light
Cadmium orange light + Payne's gray + burnt sienna
Sap green + brilliant green light + cerulean blue
Brilliant green light + cadmium yellow light + flesh

3 The white portions of the paint tubes cast blue- or violet-hued shadows and reflect the light and surrounding color. To capture these shadows and keep them interesting, I use a lot of color variation (see color samples above right) and alter the direction of my brushstrokes. I'm also careful to keep these areas loose and spontaneous by not overworking them. My goal is not to achieve strict photorealism but to create a more "painterly" quality. As with the previous steps, I work these colors into the paint while it is still wet.

4 Using a medium flat brush loaded with flesh, I fill in the highlight areas and paint around the edges of the shadows and the lettering details. I allow some of the underpainting to show through to enhance the effect of the light. Next I mix the colors for the paint tubes (see color samples above), and I add details and enhance the shadows with a little Payne's gray. I also use flesh for the white lettering on the tubes. Finally I enhance the highlighted areas of the paint tubes and caps using titanium white mixed with cadmium yellow light, cadmium orange light, flesh, and cerulean blue.

Rendering Glass

by Tom Swimm

Although you may consider painting glass a challenge, its transparent and reflective qualities make it a fun and interesting still-life subject. Glass both reflects light and allows light to travel through it, creating vivid highlights and fascinating translucent effects. And when colored glass is backlit by the sun or artificial light, the color is intensified, projecting a wide range of exciting visual effects. For this still life, Tom Swimm arranged an eclectic group of bottles of varying shapes, sizes, and colors on a glass table with backlighting. This setup creates wonderful reflections and strong contrasts of color and value.

Color Palette

alizarin crimson, brilliant green light, burnt sienna, cadmium orange light, cadmium red light, cadmium yellow light, cerulean blue, flesh, light blue-violet, medium magenta (acrylic), Payne's gray, phthalo violet, Prussian blue, raw sienna, sap green, titanium white, yellow ochre

PAINTING WHAT YOU SEE

When painting complex forms and symmetrical objects like these colored glass bottles, begin by looking at the composition as a whole, squinting your eyes to help break down the scene to its essential shapes and colors. Don't be influenced by your idea of what the glass shapes *should* look like; just study them carefully and paint only what you really see. Copy the shapes, lines, and angles, and note the color transitions where the glass objects overlap. Try turning the reference photo and the canvas upside down, to help you see the colors and shapes out of context. That way you're more likely to paint only what you truly see.

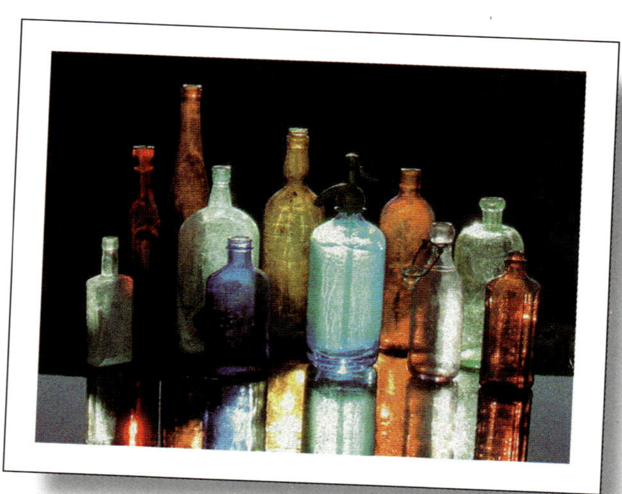

► CREATING DYNAMIC SETUPS The trick to this still life is to edit the group of bottles to achieve a good balance of shapes and colors. I was especially pleased with the graphic effect made by the reflections, creating a lively setup with a lot of visual interest and plays of light.

1 For this painting, I choose a 22" x 28" stretched canvas and begin drawing a rough outline of the bottles with a fine-tip marker. As I sketch, I'm careful to note the proportions and the relationships among the bottles, taking special care to faithfully draw their different angles and heights.

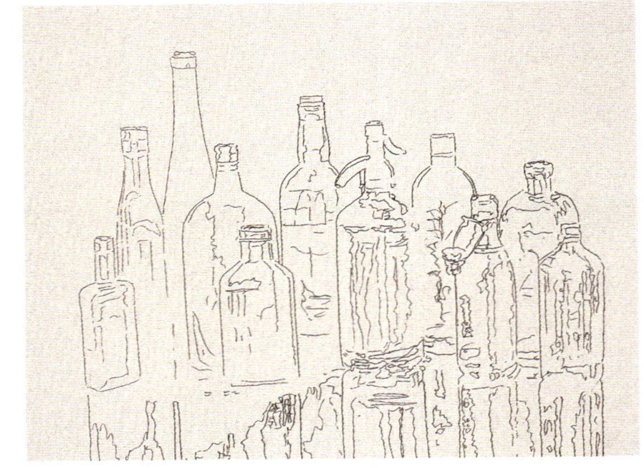

2 For the underpainting, I cover the canvas with a thin coat of medium magenta acrylic paint. (See page 6 for other base color options.) Because acrylic is a water-based paint, you can safely paint over it with oil. (But the reverse is not true; you cannot paint acrylic over oil because the oil will resist the acrylic.)

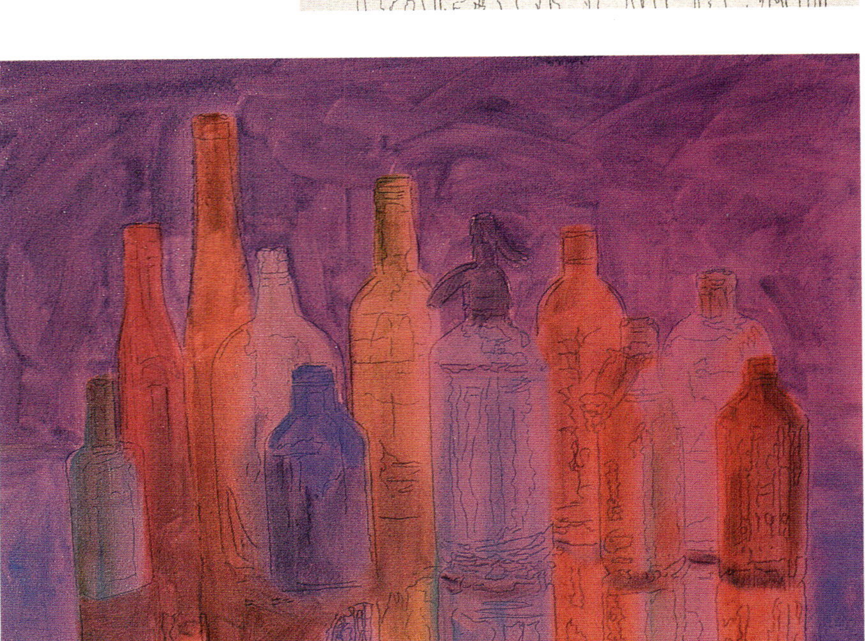

3 I start out with a limited palette of pure pigments to establish the basic colors and values. Using a large flat brush, I block in some of the shaded areas with thinned alizarin crimson, burnt sienna, raw sienna, sap green, and cerulean blue. For the background and some of the shaded areas, I also use Payne's gray. I make my brushstrokes broad and loose, keeping the paint thin enough so the drawing still shows through.

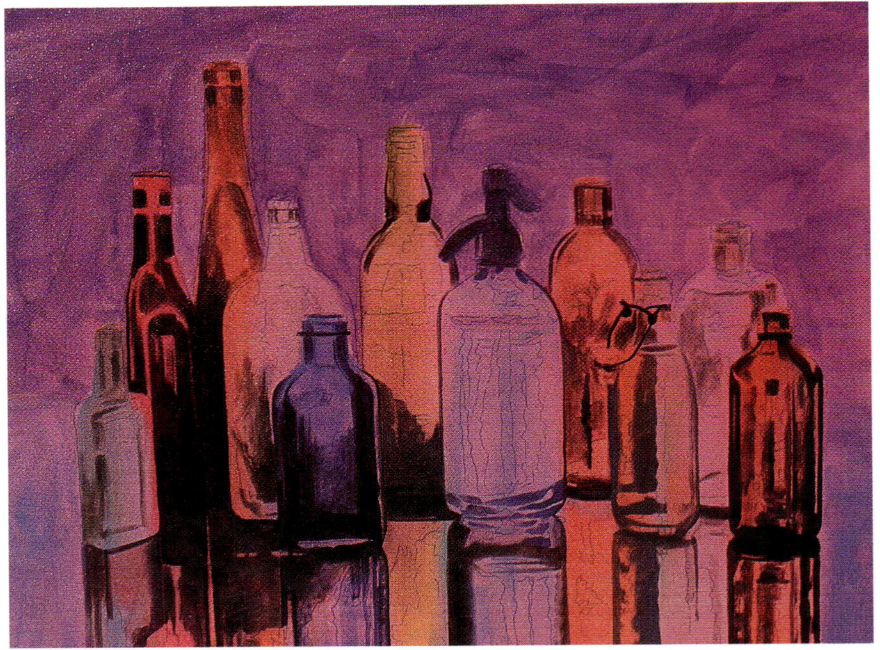

4 Next I add the details to the outlines and forms of the bottles with the edge of a medium flat brush. Here I apply the paint more thickly to establish the darkest layer of the underpainting. Then I a few details to help define each bottle and do the same thing for the reflected shapes, using Payne's gray and adding a touch of color where appropriate; for example, I add alizarin crimson for the taller bottle on the left. (See color samples on page 11.)

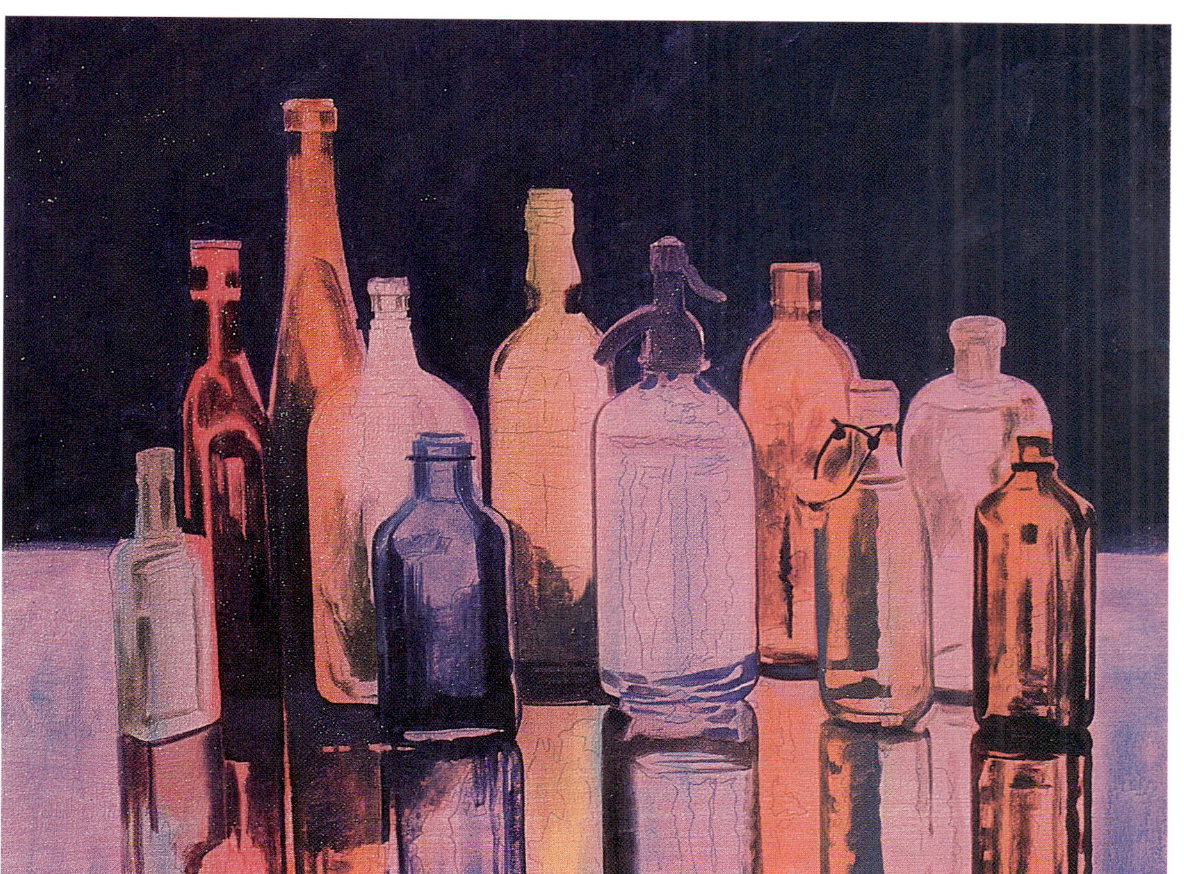

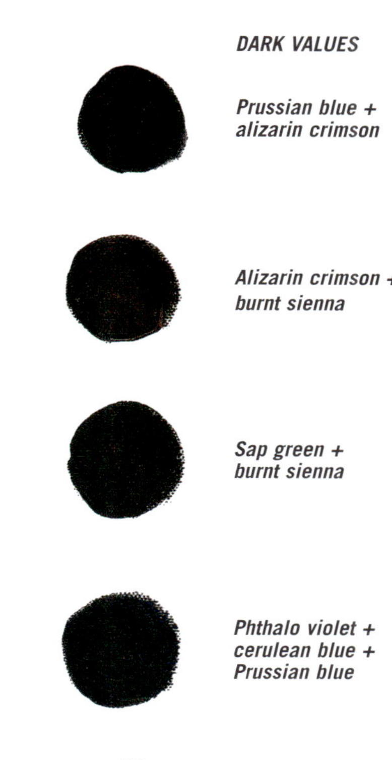

5 This step will complete the "drawing" process and establish the outlines of the bottles above the table line. For the background, I mix Prussian blue with alizarin crimson and apply the paint in thick brushstrokes, varying the angle of my brush. You can use a larger brush, but be sure to turn it on its edge to produce crisp outlines.

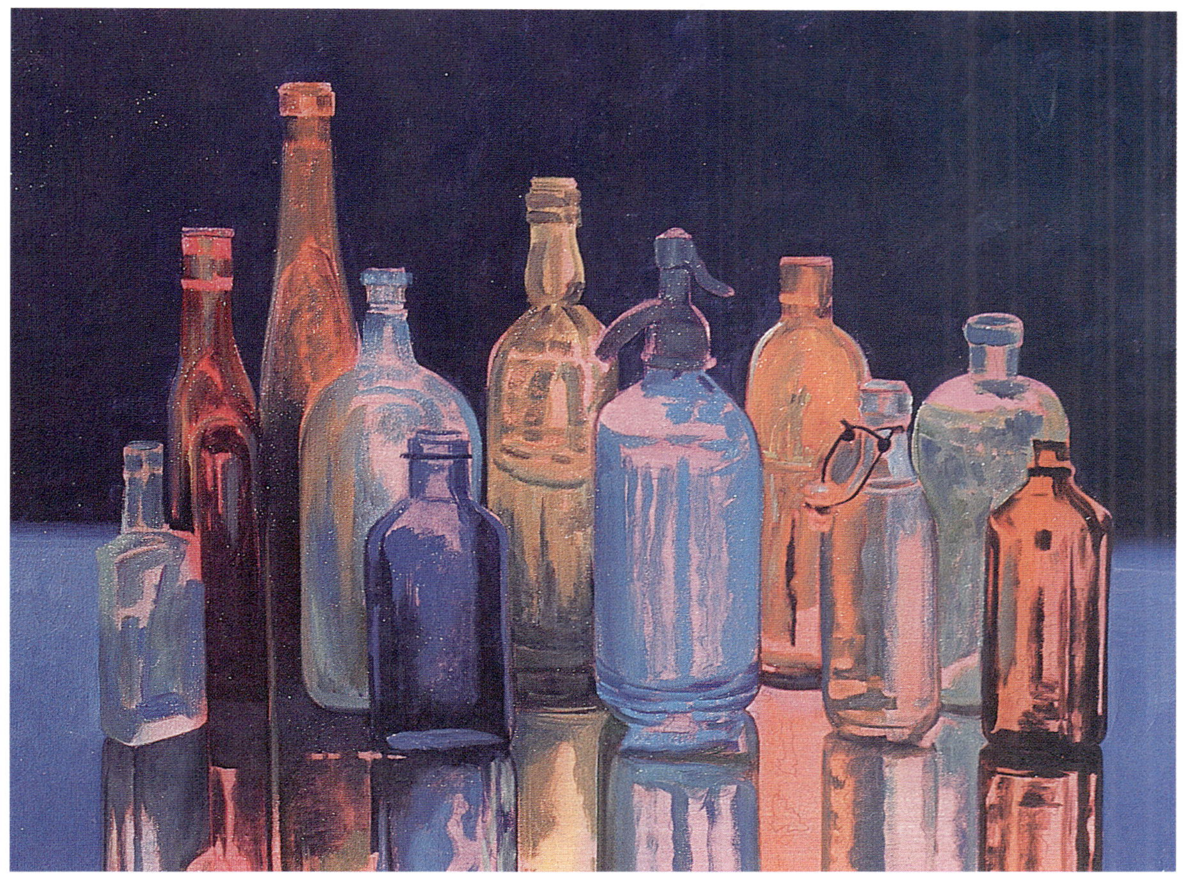

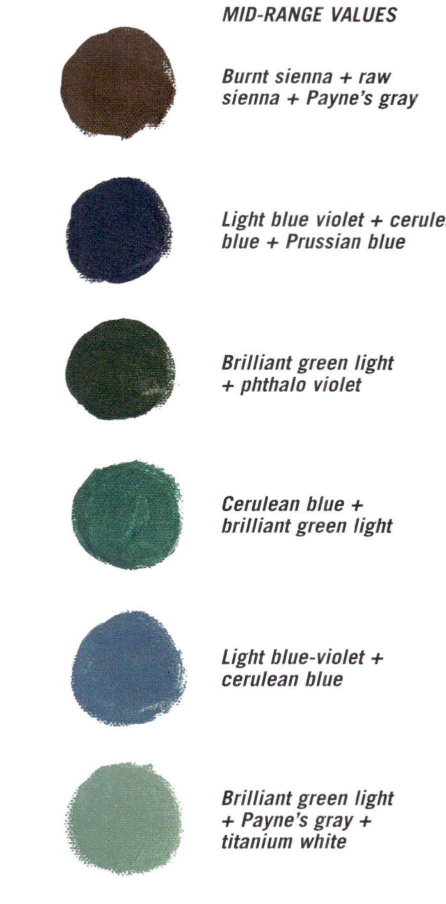

6 Now I begin adding slightly lighter values to define the color of the bottles and develop their forms. (See the color samples at right.) I also apply another layer of color to the tabletop, using cerulean blue and gradually mixing in titanium white to create a smooth gradation. Once I've finished painting the bottles themselves, I apply the same color mixtures to create the nuances in their reflections. Since the glass reflections aren't exact mirror replicas, you can improvise a lot with this step; just trust your eye and make the layers of color interesting and varied.

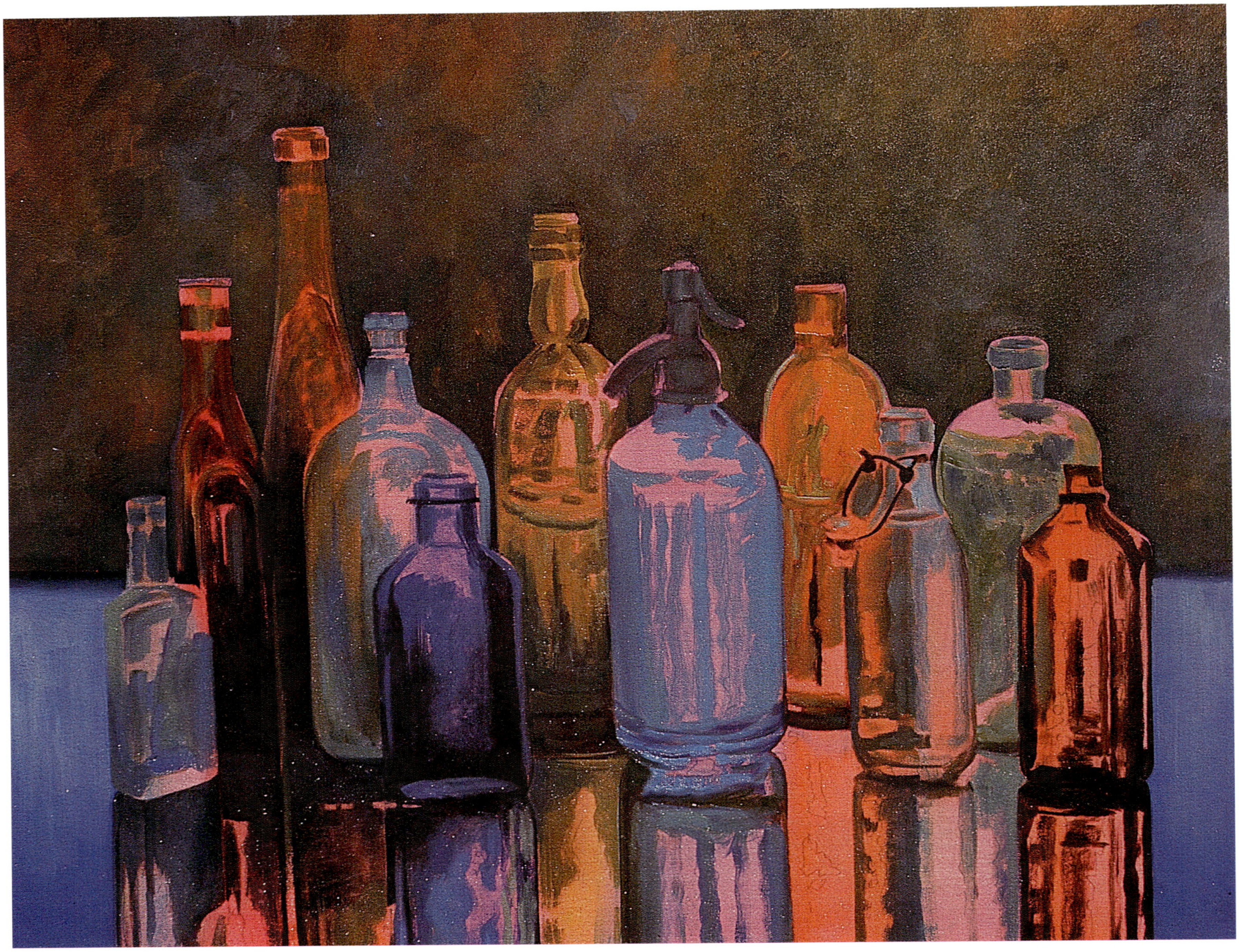

7 I begin painting the background using loose, random brushstrokes and warm mixes of cadmium red light, burnt sienna, yellow ochre, and cerulean blue. I don't plan out the background before I begin; I just let the brush and the paint do the work until I am satisfied with the result. Do the same with your painting—or try different colors for a unique effect. Remember that the beauty of oil is that the medium is opaque and flexible, enabling you to scrape off the paint and paint over an area until you're satisfied.

► **PAINTING GLASS** Clear glass has no color of its own, but it reflects the colors of the surrounding objects. Tinted glass, though colored, has a similar quality, and you can approach it in the same way. Since you can see what's behind glass, start by painting that, and then define the forms of the glass with highlights. A curved glass container distorts the shapes of the objects behind it and in it; so think in terms of shapes, colors, values, and intensity, and look for the highlights and darks that give clues to the shapes.

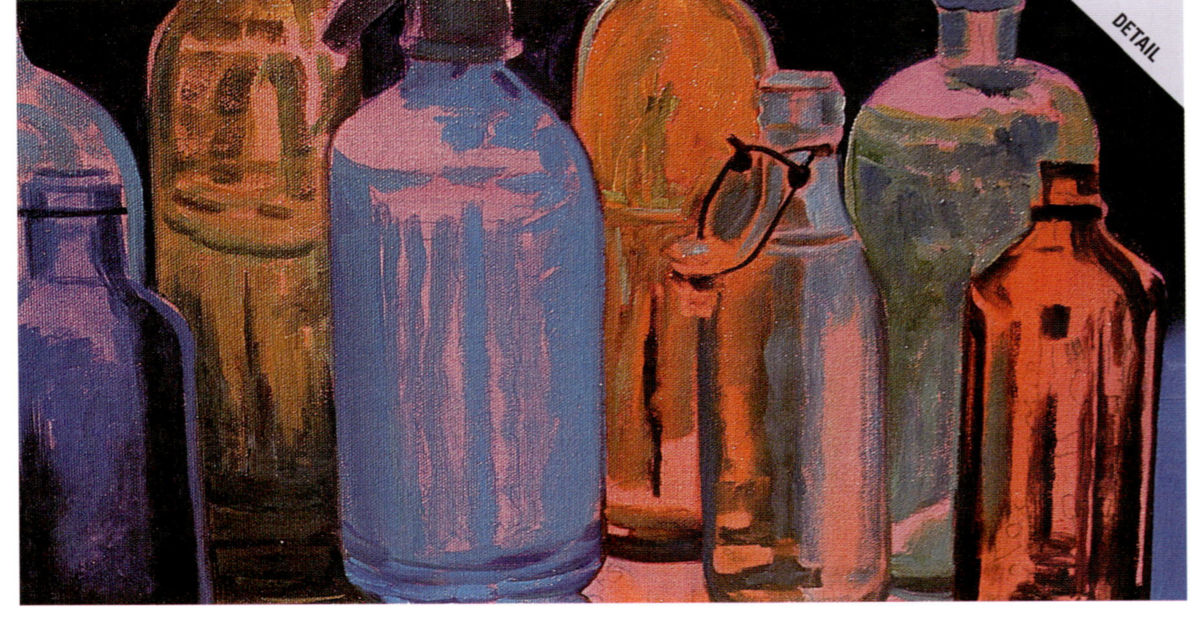

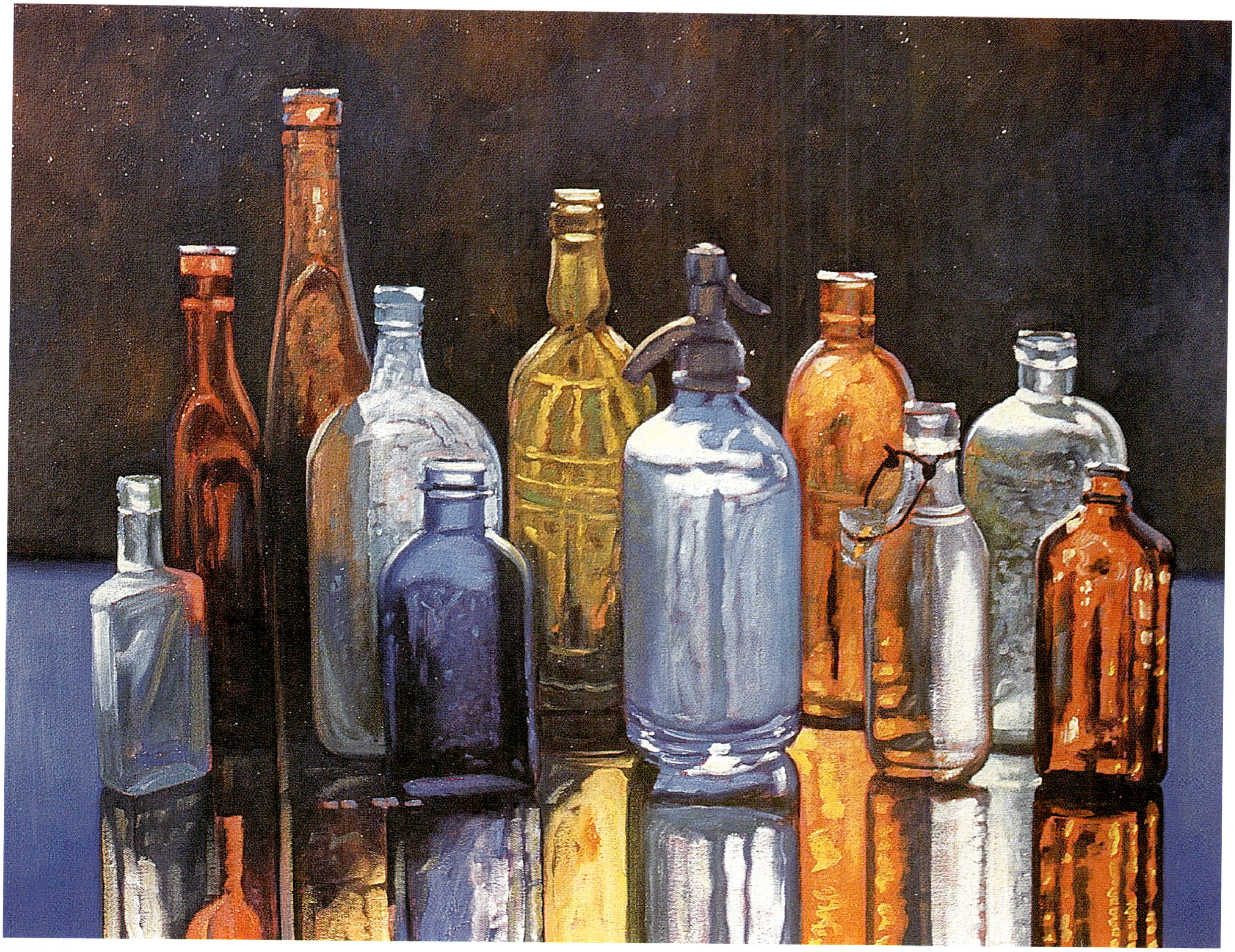

8 Now I enhance the color and light in the bottles using various light mixes of the following colors: titanium white, cadmium yellow light, cadmium orange light, flesh, yellow ochre, light blue violet, and cerulean blue. Notice that I never use white straight from the tube. Try different combinations of these mixtures and vary the color intensity; you'll be amazed at how dramatic the results will be! After I finish the larger areas, I decide to add a few pinpoint-sized highlights to the tops of the bottles.

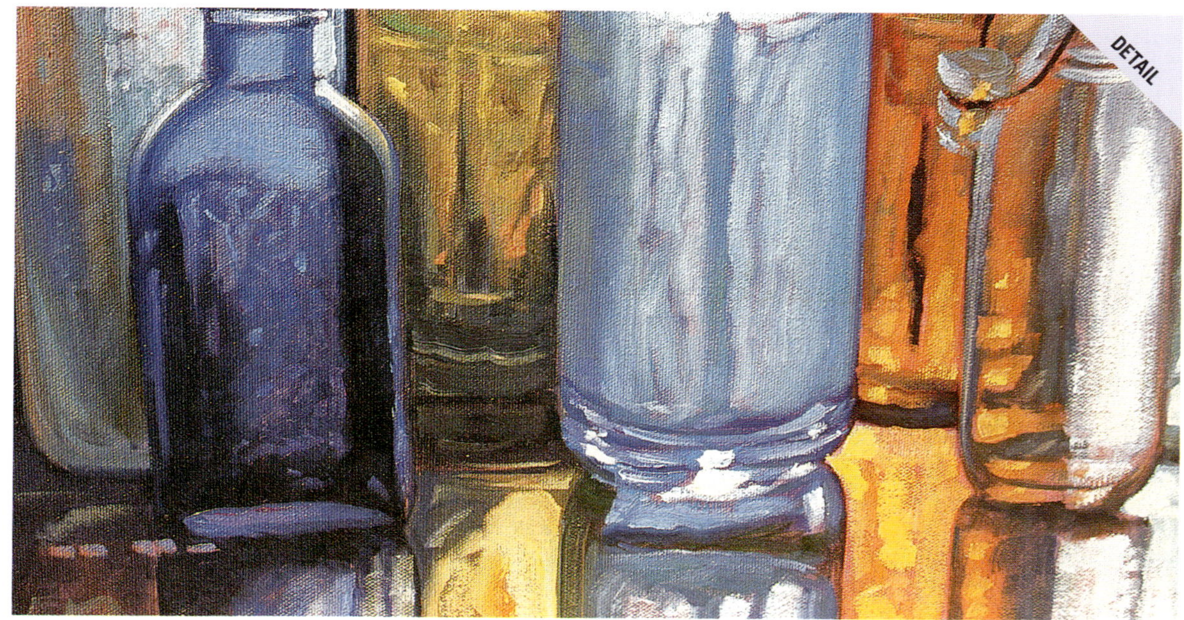

◄ **RENDERING REFLECTIONS** I paint the reflections on the glass tabletop a little more loosely and with less detail, so as not to detract from the main focus of the bottles. The color of the reflections is more intense, especially in the warmer values, so I load the brush and pull the color down from each reflected area. I'm also careful to keep the symmetry parallel, making sure the shapes of the reflections are consistent with the shapes of the bottles.

Capturing Time of Day

by Mia Tavonatti

There's no need to limit your still lifes to the indoors, especially when there are so many wonderful outdoor settings to choose from. When painting an outdoor still life, time of day becomes a significant factor, since colors, light, and shadows differ at various times of the day. There are cool hues and longer shadows in the morning and early evening, and there are warmer hues and shorter shadows at mid-day. And the warmth or coolness of the colors contributes to the emotion—or mood—your painting will convey. For example, warm, light colors (reds, yellows, and oranges) evoke excitement or passion, while cool colors (blues, greens, and violets) have a more calming effect. In this painting, artist Mia Tavonatti chose a late afternoon setting to focus on the long, dramatic shadows and the striking contrasts between the warm light and the cool shadows. All these factors create a powerful sense of drama that makes this scene so captivating.

Color Palette

alizarin crimson, burnt sienna, cadmium orange light, cadmium red light, cadmium yellow light, Payne's gray, phthalo blue, sap green, ultramarine blue, yellow ochre, zinc white

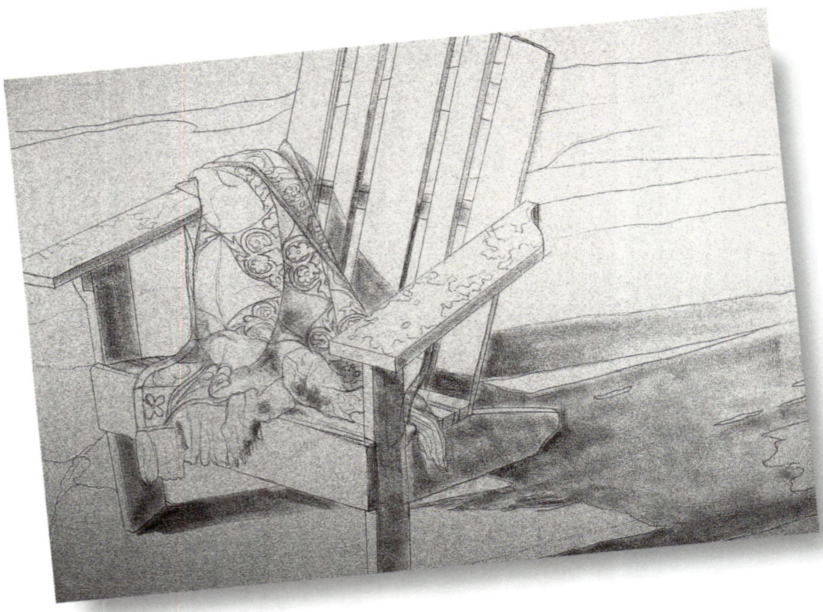

STARTING WITH A SKETCH Before I begin painting, I make a careful drawing to establish the basic shapes. Here I shade in the darkest shadows as a guide for the subsequent application of color. (I photocopied a reference photo to create a guide for my sketch, but you can also draw freehand.) I deliberately crop the chair at the top, left, and bottom so that it fills the space, resulting in less background and a more striking composition. Then, before painting, I spray the drawing with a workable fixative to keep it from smudging.

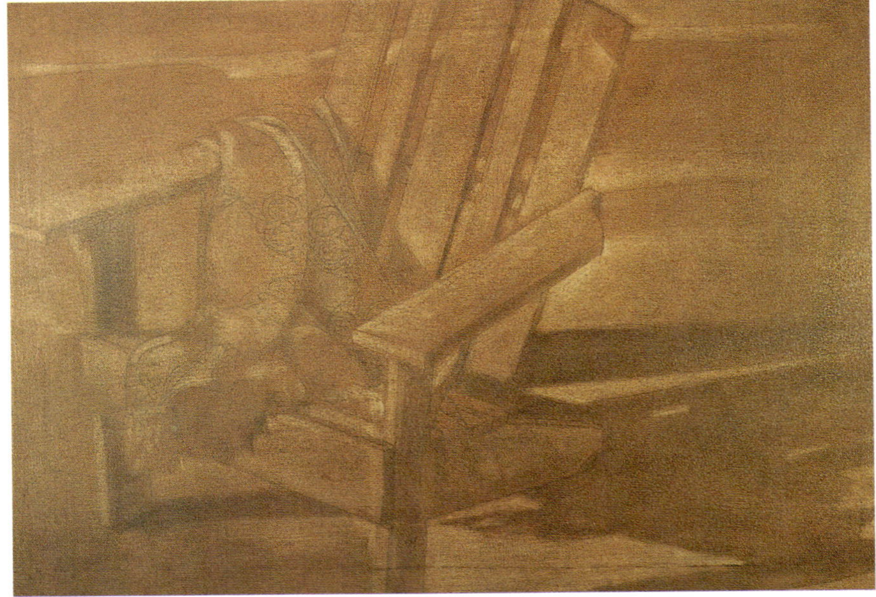

1 Using a large flat brush, I cover the entire canvas with a wash of burnt sienna and sap green. Then I gently rub the surface with a soft cotton rag so the color is even and I can see my drawing through the paint. To establish the lightest values, I remove more color in the areas of strongest light. I want the base wash to help unify all the colors in the painting, so I'm careful not to remove too much color from any one place. You can use any thinner, but I mix my own medium using 1/5 damar varnish, 1/5 linseed oil, and 3/5 turpentine or odorless mineral spirits.

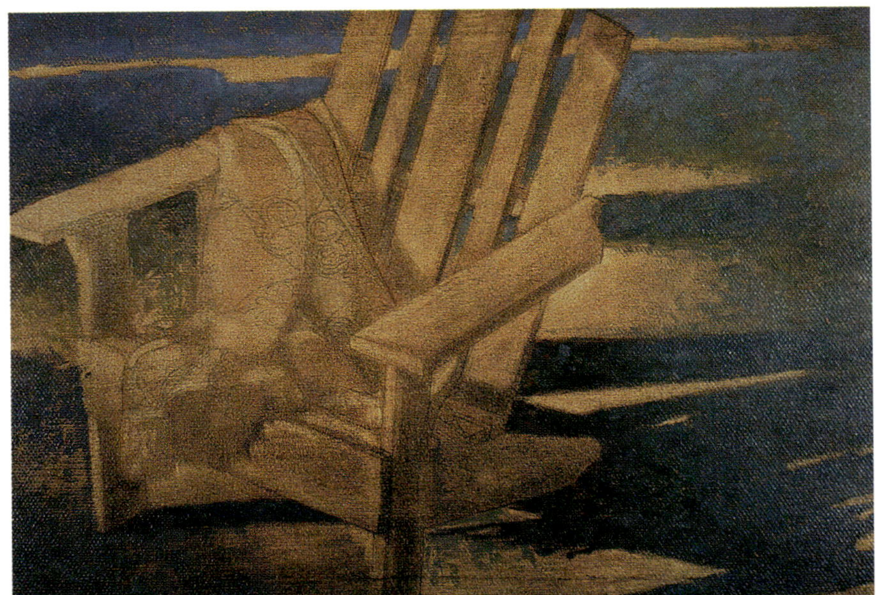

2 Next I lay in the background and shadow colors. For the cast shadows on the concrete, I use small and medium flat brushes with short, square strokes. For the cool, darker shadows on the left, I apply ultramarine blue, phthalo blue, and white. As I move to the right, I lighten and warm the mixture with white and yellow ochre. I also graduate from dark, rich values in the foreground to cool, light values in the background, adding to the sense of depth. Next I add cadmium red light to the concrete around the legs of the chair to show the chair's reflected color.

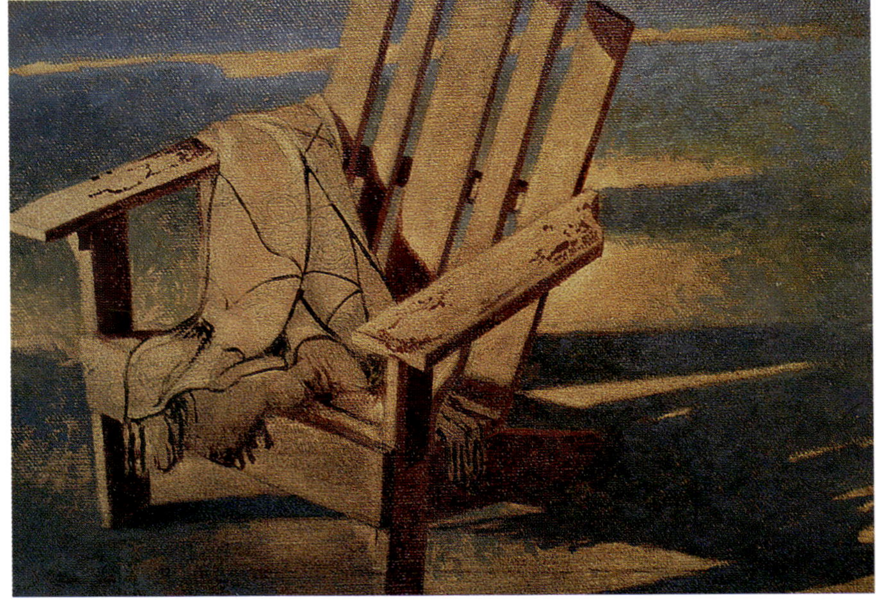

3 With this painting, I've been applying color from dark to light; this way I can gradually build up the depth of my colors as my painting progresses. At this stage, most of the mid-range values have been established, and I'm ready to add the darkest shadows to the chair itself. Using a detail brush, I carefully lay in the dark, cool, red shadows with a mixture of alizarin crimson, cadmium red light, and zinc white. For the darkest shadows, I add a small amount of phthalo blue to the mixture.

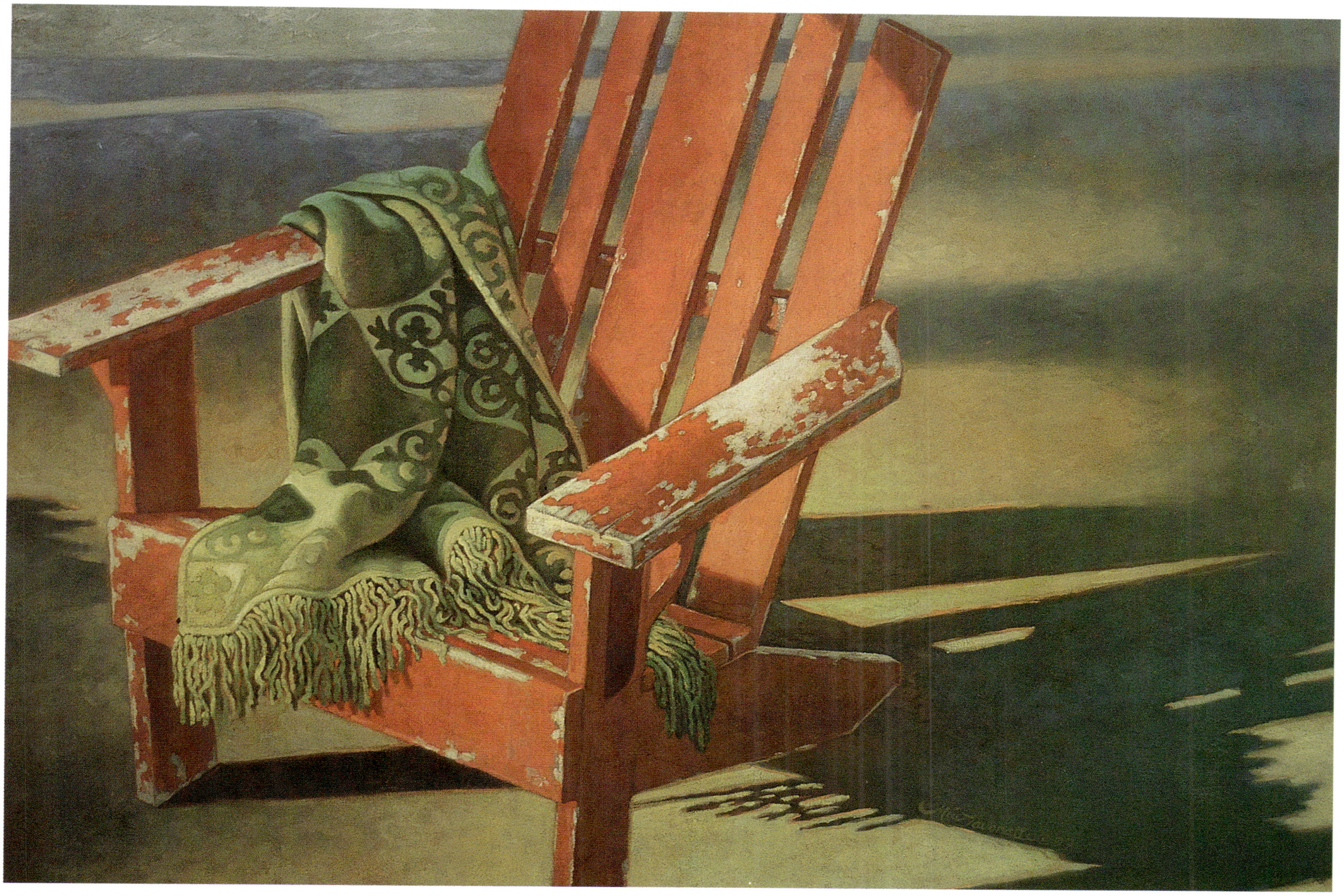

6 Next I finish the chair, using both flat and round brushes to fill in the red painted areas. To produce the chipped wood effect, I let the undercolor show through in some areas for an aged, worn appearance; I concentrate these areas along the edges of the chair's planks. Then I finish the blanket; I use the shadow colors plus touches of white and yellow ochre, and I gradually lighten the color as it rolls over the blanket folds. To further convey the blanket's soft texture, I use small strokes of paint that I blend very little.

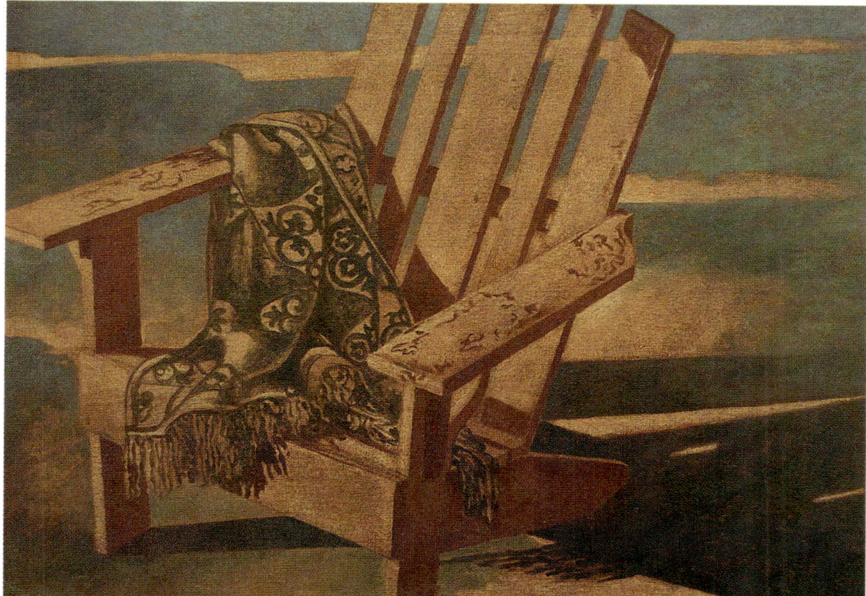

4 Next I build up the shadows and begin to establish the blanket's detail. Using the same small detail brush, I paint the shadows and the dark areas of the blanket pattern using sap green mixed with phthalo blue and lightened with cadmium orange light. By substituting orange for white, I maintain the warmth of my colors—in keeping with the warm afternoon light. I use brighter values of the orange mixture in the backs of the blanket folds that are hit by the chair's reflected red light.

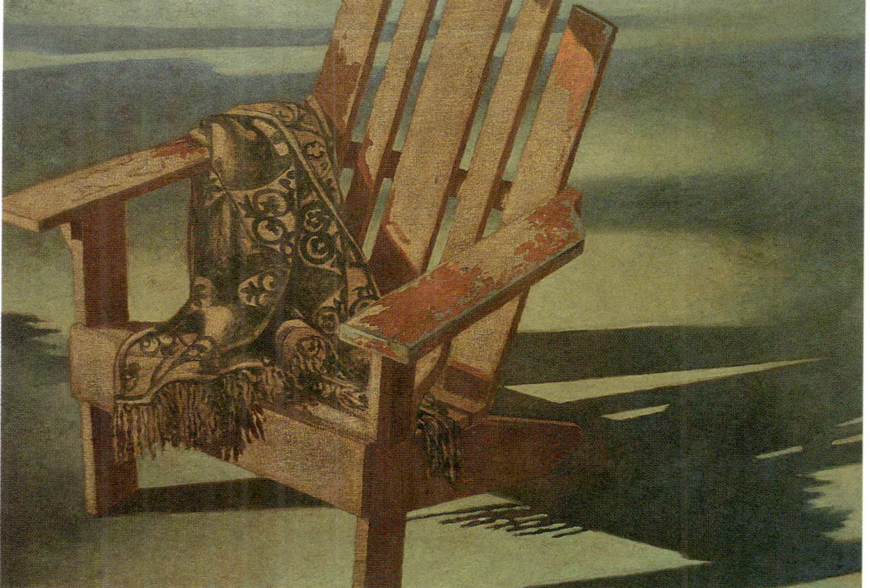

5 After finishing the shadows, I move on to the lighter, brighter areas. For the concrete, I use the shadow colors warmed with white and yellow ochre, creating the contrast between light and shadow. For the cracks and peeling paint on the chair, I use a detail brush and alternate between a mix of Payne's gray, white, and yellow ochre (where the red paint has peeled away) and a brighter mix of cadmium red light, white, and cadmium yellow light (where the paint remains). Then I darken the edges of the paint chips with a little Payne's gray or alizarin crimson.

Depicting Textures

by Mia Tavonatti

Including texture in your painting is a great way to add a sense of realism. Artists often create the *illusion* of texture, but they may also play up the physical texture found in the grain of the canvas or made by the brush's bristles. Texture can also be produced by applying the paint in different ways, such as using smooth strokes for shiny objects and thicker applications for rough surfaces. In this simple yet innovative composition, artist Mia Tavonatti chose fruits with varied and interesting textures—from the even texture of the papaya skin to the rough exterior of the pineapple. Even the concrete surface where the artist placed the fruit has a course texture, drawing attention to the interesting shapes of the shadows that connect the pieces of fruit into a cohesive unit.

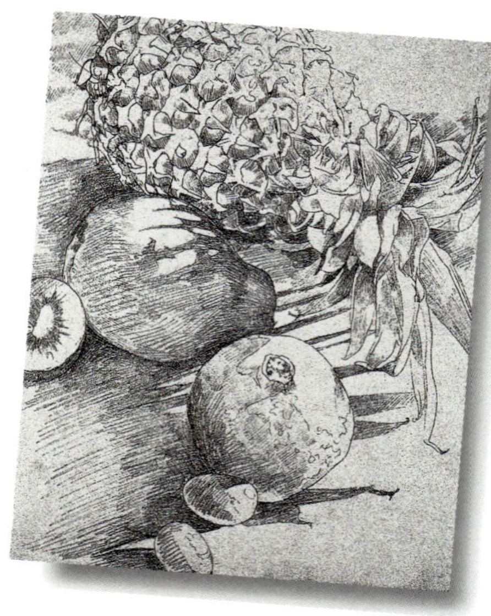

CROPPING IN In my initial sketch, I crop the drawing on all four sides to make the fruit appear larger and more detailed. I also establish the main shadows on the ground and on the pineapple. Because these areas are more complex, I want to make sure they are accurate from the beginning.

Color Palette

alizarin crimson, black, burnt sienna, cadmium orange medium, cadmium red light, cadmium yellow light, Indian red, magenta, Payne's gray, permanent green, phthalo green, phthalo yellow-green, Prussian blue, purple madder, red ochre, sap green, ultramarine blue, yellow ochre, zinc white

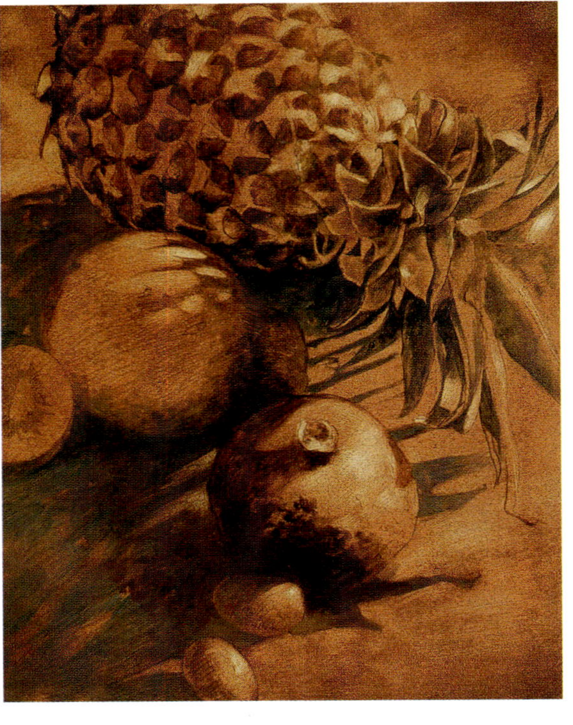

1 After toning the canvas with a thin layer of burnt sienna with a touch of sap green, I lay in the darkest shadow colors. For the pineapple's cast shadows, I use a small flat brush and darker mixes of burnt sienna and sap green. Next I render the papaya's shadow with sap green and yellow ochre. For the pomegranate, I use sap green and red ochre and sap green and alizarin crimson; the miniature oranges are cadmium orange medium with a touch of sap green. Then I mix black and white for the gray concrete, adding yellow ochre for warm green-gray areas and red ochre for warm red-grays. For the cool grays, I add Prussian blue and magenta. Next I add grayer versions of the fruit colors in their cast shadows.

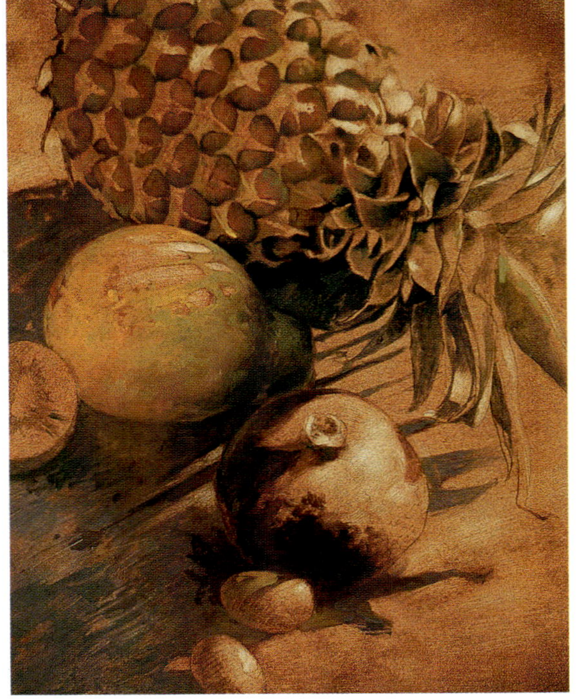

2 Now that the shadows are defined, I slowly graduate my colors from dark to light to smooth the transitions that help convey the roundness of the forms. Using my small flat brush, I lay in the dark to mid-range values on the pineapple with various mixes of burnt sienna, cadmium red light, and cadmium orange, darkened with sap green. I also use mixes of these same colors for the papaya. In contrast to the smooth gradations on the pineapple, I use short strokes and very little blending to create the rough texture of the papaya.

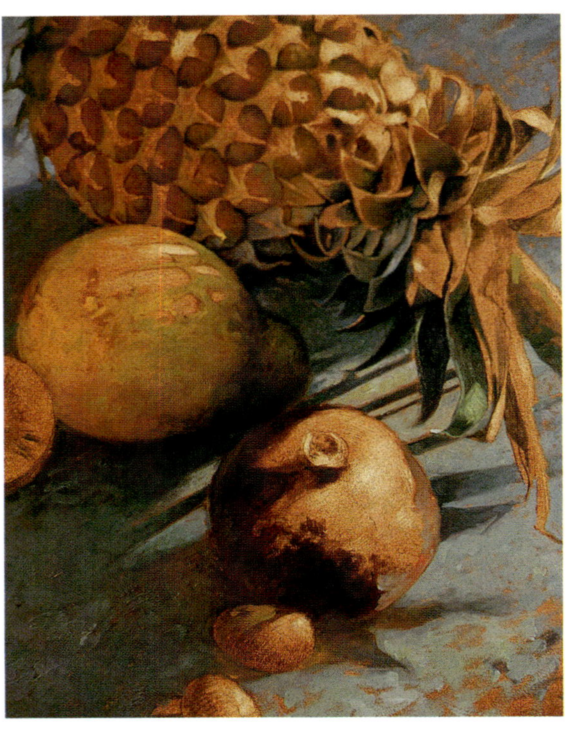

3 Next I work the adjacent areas wet-into-wet, blurring the edges of the fruits as they recede into the shadows and leaving more defined edges where the light hits. Using a small round brush, I paint the cool, dark green leaves with phthalo green and permanent green, darkened sometimes with ultramarine blue and sometimes with black or sap green. For the purples on the leaves, I use mixes of Indian red, Payne's gray, and white. For the light concrete in the foreground, I warm the gray shadow colors with white and yellow ochre. Then I use a small flat brush and short, choppy strokes to apply added texture.

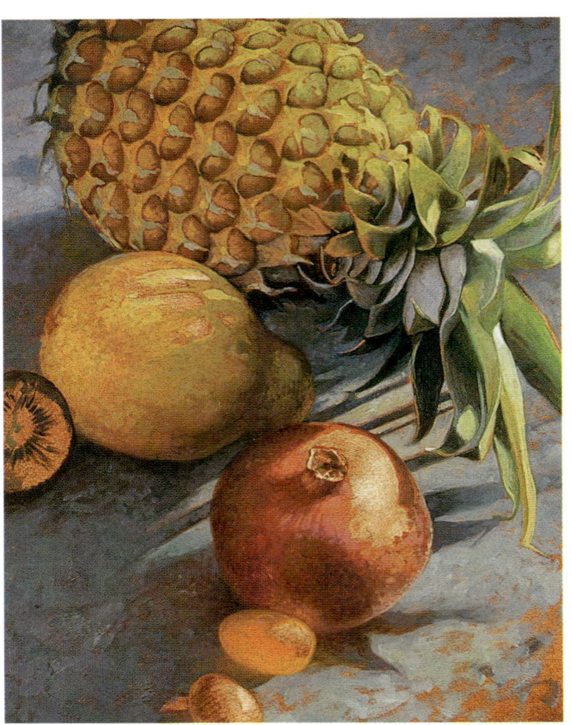

4 For the mid-range values of the pomegranate, I use both purple madder and alizarin crimson, each lightened with cadmium red light, cadmium orange, and yellow ochre. Then I mix sap green and cadmium red light to add texture to the main shadow and along the left side. Next I paint the pineapple nodules with cadmium red light and cadmium orange, darkened with sap green; I lighten the mix with phthalo yellow-green and white toward the right. I also add the lighter purples to the backs of the shadowed leaves using magenta, Payne's gray, and white. Where the leaves are more translucent, I use sap green mixed with phthalo yellow-green and phthalo yellow, adding more yellow and white for the lightest areas.

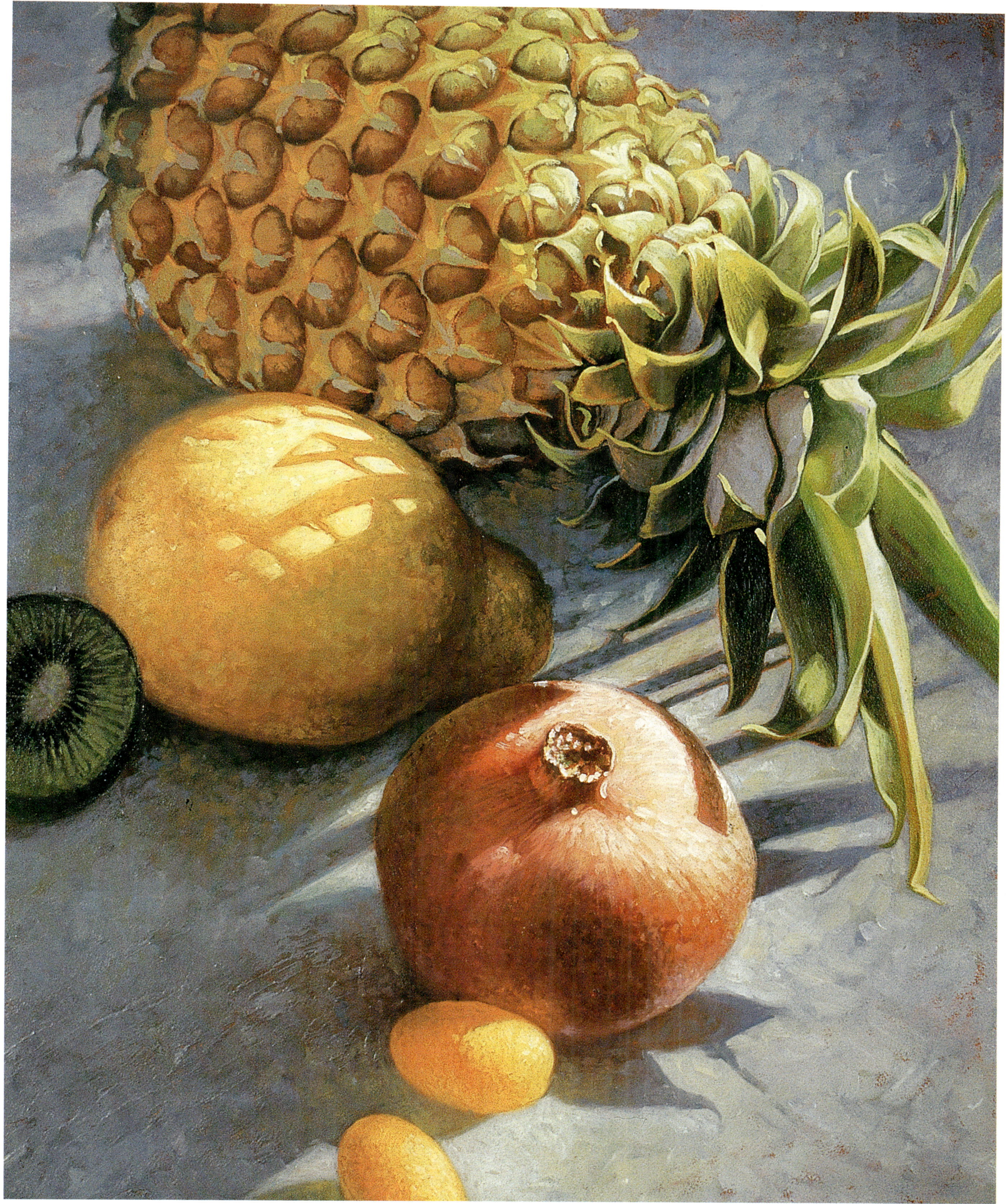

5 Next I move on to the light falling across the fruit. I use mostly cadmium orange and cadmium yellow light lightened with zinc white to finish molding the forms of the papaya and oranges. For the pomegranate, I use a small round brush and cadmium red light, cadmium orange medium, and cadmium yellow light (each lightened with zinc white), brightening the bottom with a medium pink mix of alizarin crimson and zinc white. For the kiwi, I use permanent green mixed with black (with a little orange for warmth) for the fruit and pure black for the seeds. Using a fine-point brush and gradations of phthalo yellow-green, cadmium yellow light, and zinc white, I lay in the highlights on the leaves and pineapple without blending to create the look of texture. Next I refine and soften the edges of the leaves by tracing around them with the background grays and my detail brush. Then I switch to a larger brush and refine and lighten some of the shadows. Finally I apply various light grays mixed with zinc white, black, and yellow ochre or magenta into the lightest areas around the oranges and pomegranate.

Playing with Patterns

by Mia Tavonatti

Even though still lifes are composed of inanimate objects, they are by no means lifeless! A lively still life is one that engages the eye, inviting the viewer in and around the painting. (See "Setting Up a Still Life" on page 4.) And—as with adding texture—including patterned elements contributes a great deal of interest to a still life. In this charming breakfast setup, Mia pulls the eye in by placing the coffee cup slightly off the bottom of the picture plane. Then she leads the viewer around a visual path of patterns, from the checkered napkin to the striped pastry and then to the lace doily at the top. And the contrasts between the patterned elements and the smooth, green stoneware are accentuated by Mia's repeated pairings of red and green *complements*—colors opposite one other on the color wheel. These complementary colors add a vibrant, energetic feeling to what might otherwise be a static setting.

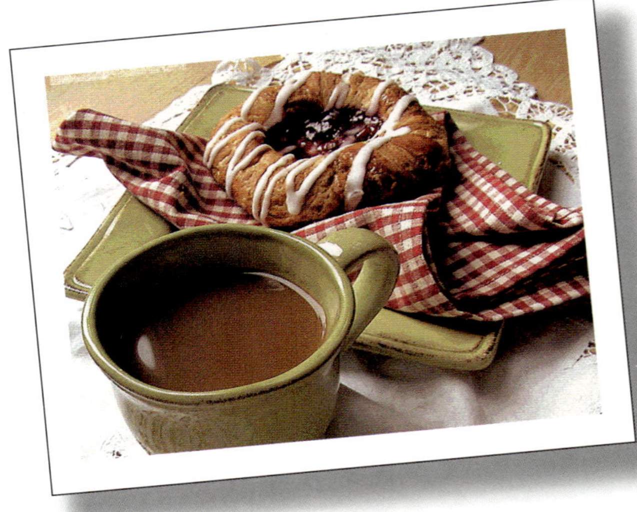

◀ **COMBINING ELEMENTS** Even the simplest subject can be made fascinating by taking an unusual viewpoint. This photo was taken from above and at an angle, tightly focusing on the main elements. This viewpoint—along with the coupling of red's complement, green—brings attention to both red and white patterns in the cloth and in the Danish.

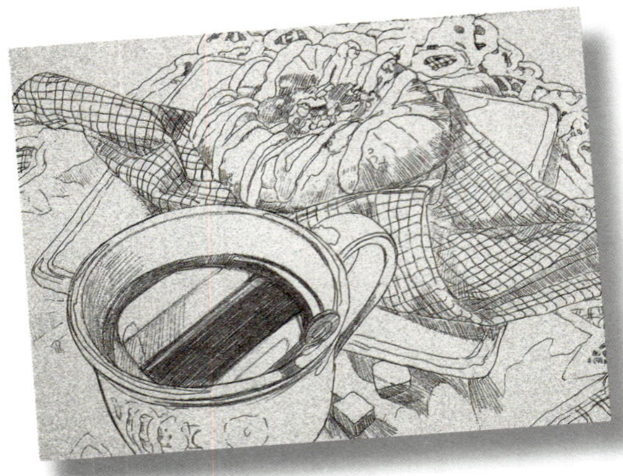

PREPARING THE SKETCH To test the overall composition of my still life, I draw an initial sketch on a sheet of paper; this allows me to visualize the painting and to adjust the composition as needed before I begin painting. For example, I decided the spoon in the sketch makes the scene seem too busy, so I remove it from the painting. When I'm happy with the composition, I transfer the image to my support using carbon paper.

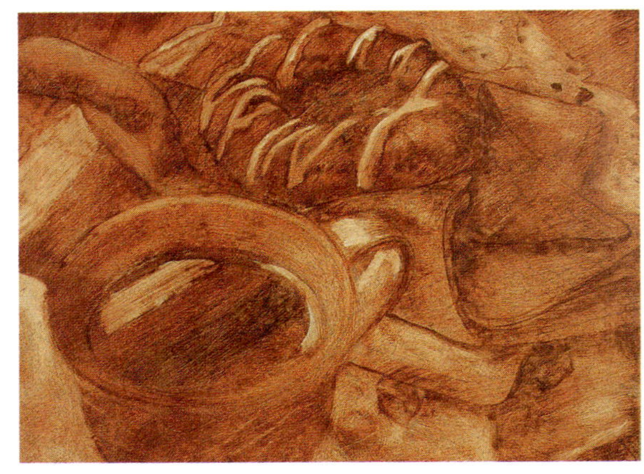

1 First I use a large flat brush to apply a base of thinned burnt sienna with a little sap green. Then I thin and even the color with a cotton rag, allowing the underlying drawing to show through. I also darken some of the lines and shadows with a small, pointed brush. Since it can be difficult to cover the dark base color with whites, I remove some color from what will be the lightest areas in my composition.

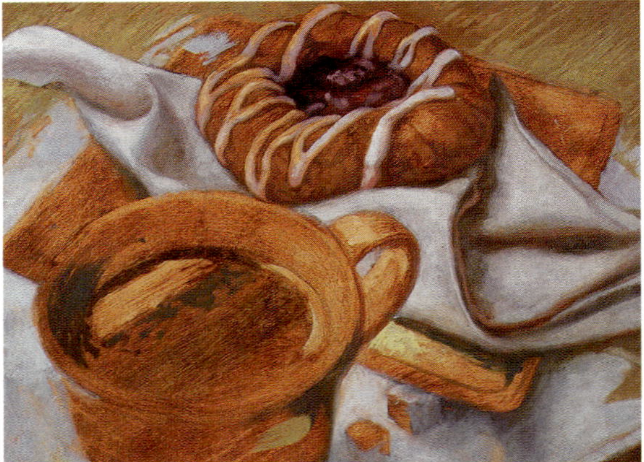

2 I paint frosting and cloth shadows with mixes of Payne's gray, magenta, and ultramarine blue, adding alizarin crimson for red tones. For the lace and napkin, I mix white with alizarin crimson for cool tints and with cad. red lt. for warms. I also mix white with various blues and magenta for blue and purple tones. For greener values, I add yellow ochre. I paint the table with yellow ochre and burnt sienna, adding white and cad. red light for lighter values.

Color Palette

alizarin crimson, burnt sienna, cadmium red light, cadmium yellow light, cerulean blue, magenta, Payne's gray, permanent green, phthalo green, sap green, ultramarine blue, white, yellow ochre

WARM GREENS
Yellow ochre + permanent green + white

COOL GREENS
Yellow ochre + permanent green + cerulean blue
Yellow ochre + permanent green + phthalo green

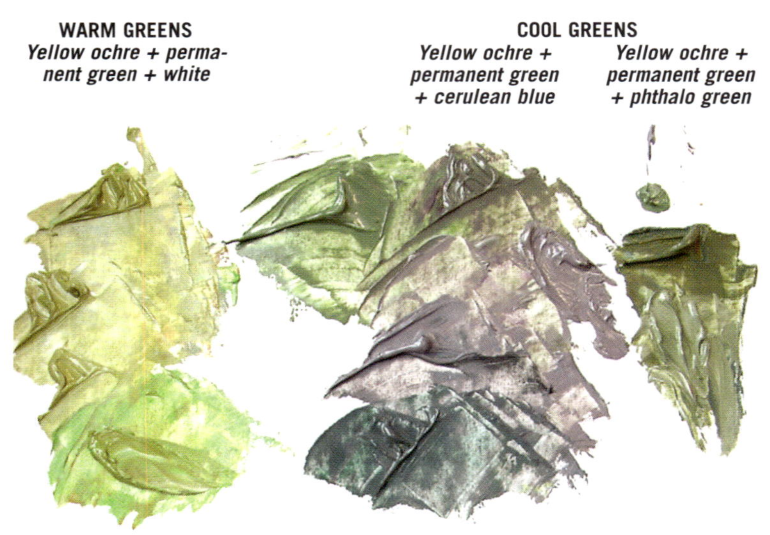

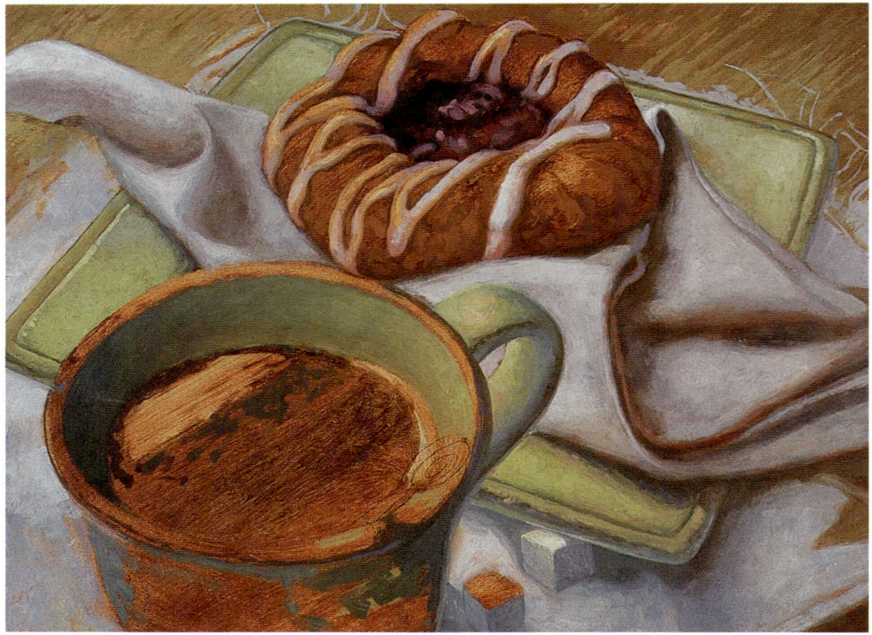

3 In this step, I begin establishing the greens, which will provide a complementary contrast to the red tones. (See color samples at left.) For the plate and coffee cup, I use a mixture of yellow ochre, permanent green, and white, graduating from cool greens in the background to warmer, sharper greens in the foreground; the gradation makes the plate appear to recede in the composition. The shadow areas and edges of the plate have many light purple values reflected from the white cloth, so for these areas I cool the mix with cerulean blue in some places and with phthalo green in others. I wait to paint the cup until I have completed the white cloth behind it.

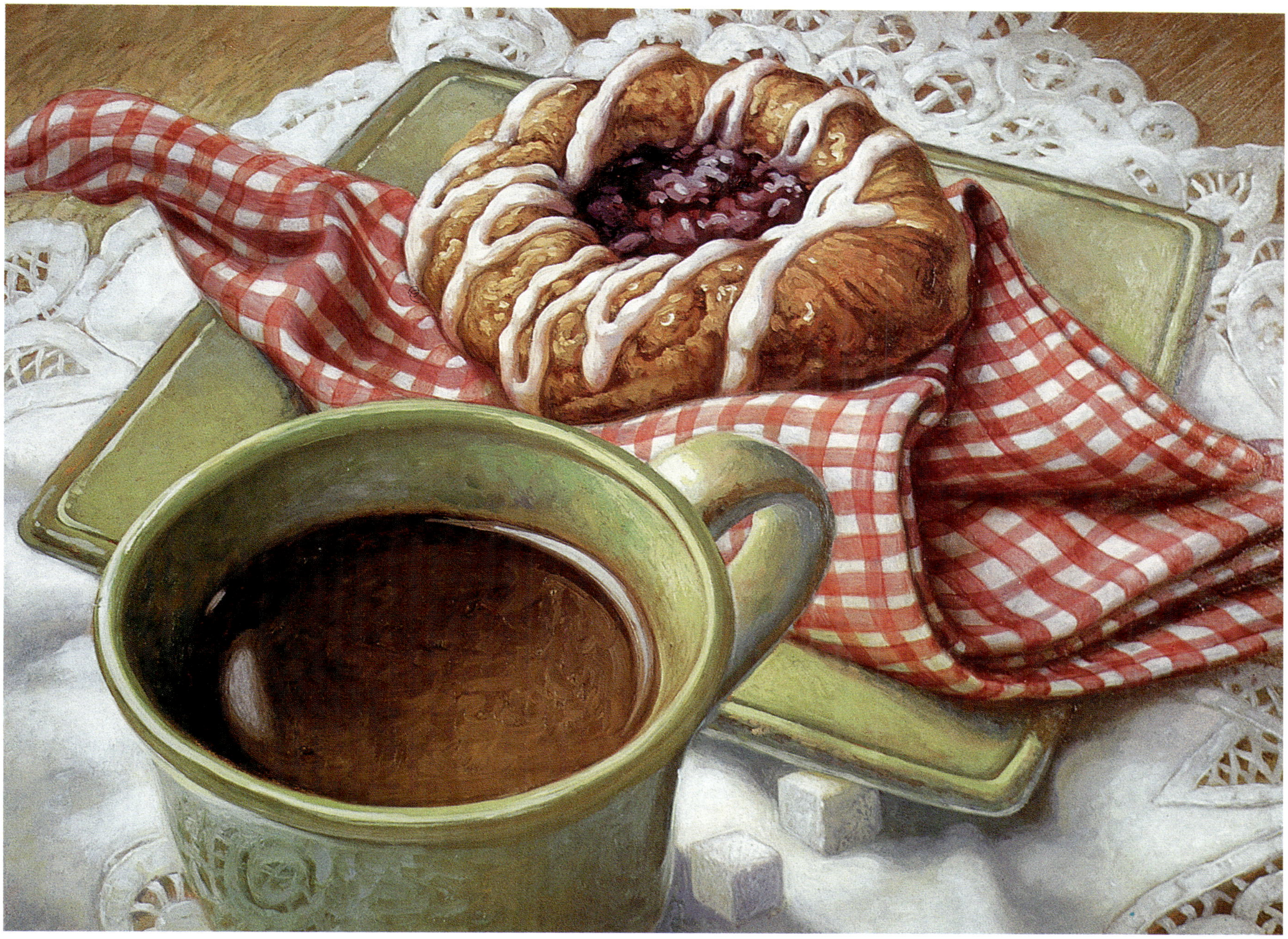

6 My final step is to create the napkin's repeating check pattern. When the whites are completely dry, I create thinned layers (*glazes*) by adding alizarin crimson and a little cadmium red to a glaze medium. I begin with the lighter stripes, adding very small amounts of the reds to the glaze medium and applying the mix with a small flat brush. I start applying the paint in the shadow areas, carefully following the folds with the stripes. I allow the first stripes to dry before painting the overlapping ones. (The dark squares are created by the two layers of paint where the stripes overlap.) Now I paint a second, darker layer, and then I use a detail brush to trace along the edges of some of the stripes, softening and blending them into the cloth at the darkest areas.

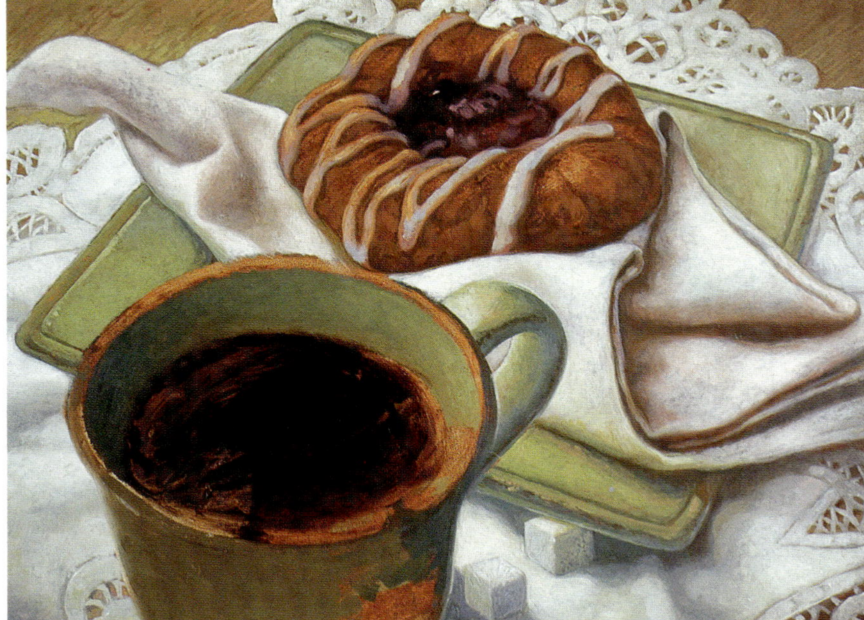

4 For the checked napkin pattern, I use very bright whites, adding cadmium yellow for warmer values and cadmium red for pinker ones. Using a small round brush, I *scumble* the paint into the lightest areas. (To scumble, wipe off the excess paint from a dry paintbrush and rub or burnish the paint over the dry base color.) This technique allows the layers underneath to show through, creating smooth gradations of value. Using a detail brush, I fill in the areas of the lace pattern using the same shadow whites I used for the napkin; the shadows are very purple and cooler at the back of the painting and warmer and more colorful toward the front. Finally—with a very small flat brush—I build the highlights with small strokes, suggesting the detail in the lace.

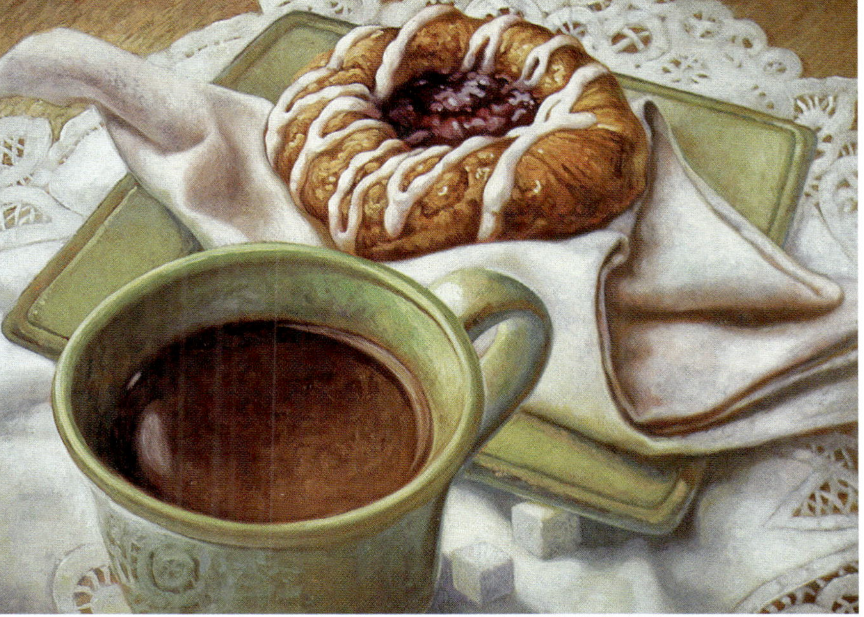

5 I begin painting the pastry using mixes of burnt sienna, yellow ochre, and cadmium red light, adding white and more yellow ochre for the lightest areas. Then I "punch up" the frosting whites with the same mixtures used for the lace, adding more reds and peaches around the shadows to reflect the pastry color. Next I continue developing the coffee cup with more intense variations of the greens in the plate. For the lace reflections on the cup, I use a brighter purple-white on the left and fade to a darker bluish-white toward the center. For the coffee colors, I use sap green and burnt sienna in the darkest areas, with orange added on the lighter, right side. Using a detail brush, I paint the highlights a purple-white.

Choosing Nontraditional Subjects

by Mia Tavonatti

For many beginners, choosing a still life subject can be a challenge: They just can't think of anything to paint! But deciding what to paint is one of the best parts of the creative process, allowing you to express your own personal style. And more important, you have the opportunity to choose a subject that has meaning to you.

UNCOVERING THE UNEXPECTED

When choosing a subject for a still life, you don't have to limit yourself to traditional subjects, such as a bouquet of flowers or a bowl of fruit. It's amazing how everyday objects that might go ignored—like a pile of firewood stacked against an old fence, a dried seed pod, an abandoned toy, or even a squashed can—can turn into a great still-life painting. And often a fantastic subject can be discovered right in your own neighborhood—or even in your closet! Here Mia Tavonatti created a fascinating and colorful still life from what appears to be nothing more than a random scattering of sandals. But her delightful painting is actually a careful arrangement of shapes, colors, and shadows.

▶ **ARRANGING THE ELEMENTS** When I designed this still life, my main interest was in the numerous patterns on the shoes, the design created by the arrangement of the sandals, and the shadows that fell across the shoes and the tile floor. The two white sandals provide light and color, and a rest area for the eyes.

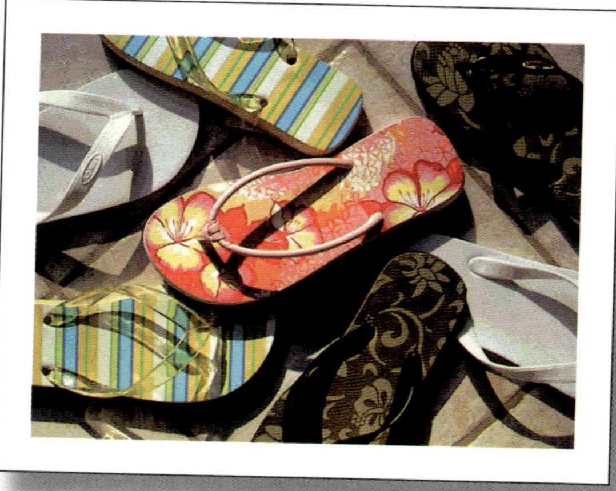

Color Palette

alizarin crimson, black, burnt sienna, cadmium orange, cadmium red light, cadmium yellow medium, cerulean blue, dioxazine purple, olive green, sap green, ultramarine blue, yellow ochre, zinc white

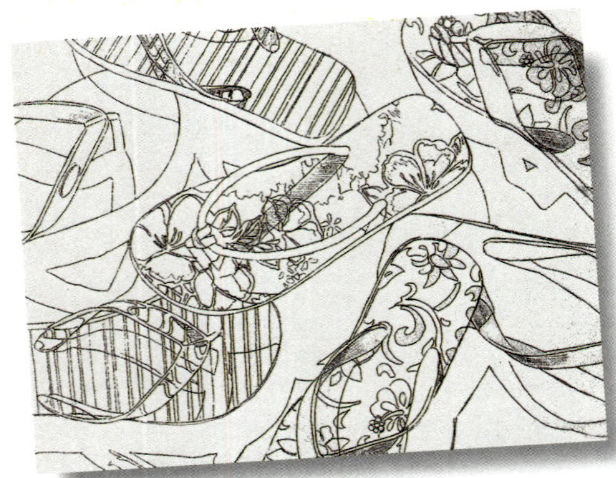

CREATING A DETAILED DRAWING Some artists make quick, rough sketches to establish the basic shapes of a setup. But I prefer to take my time to carefully duplicate the details, especially when my still life involves intricate patterns.

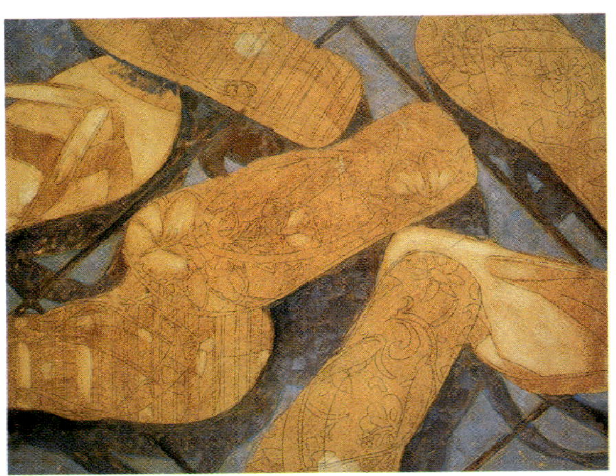

1 After underpainting with a thin wash of burnt sienna and a little sap green, I begin the dark gray cast shadows using mixes that reflect the cooler values of the sandal colors: black, white, alizarin crimson, ultramarine blue, and cerulean blue.

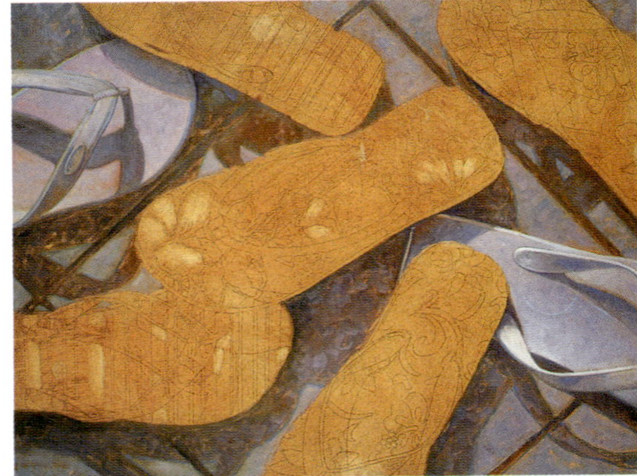

2 Next I paint the white sandals with mixes of white, ultramarine blue, and cerulean blue, adding a little alizarin crimson for the cool purples. Then I use a detail brush and thinned paint to trace over the strap edges until they're clean and smooth.

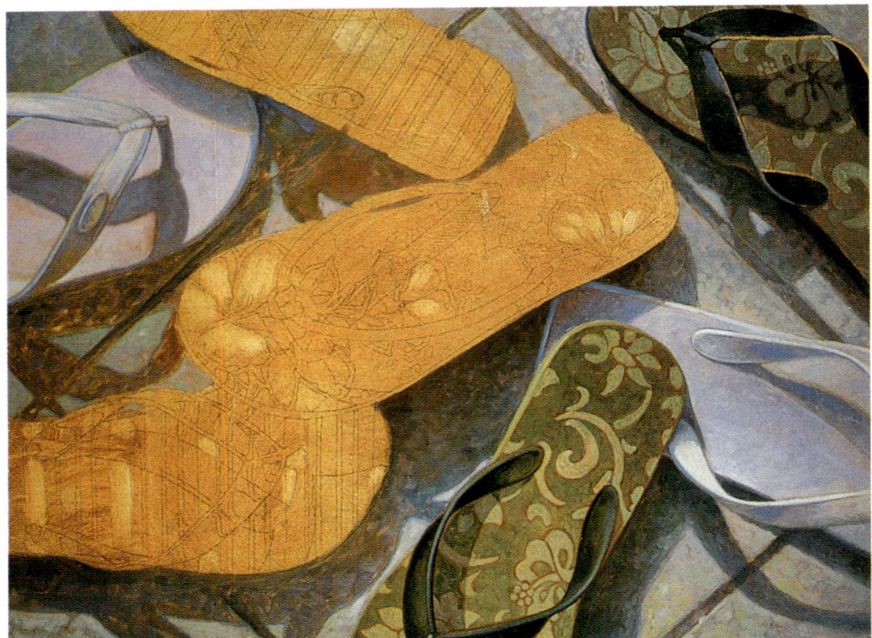

3 For the dark pattern on the green sandals, I use a flat brush to paint olive greens (black, cadmium yellow medium, and white) and peaches (cadmium red light, yellow ochre, and white). I trace the outline of the lighter pattern with cadmium red light and then paint it with lighter versions of the same greens and peaches. I lighten the black for the straps with cerulean blue and cadmium yellow medium. Then I add white to the shadow and base colors of the light gray floor.

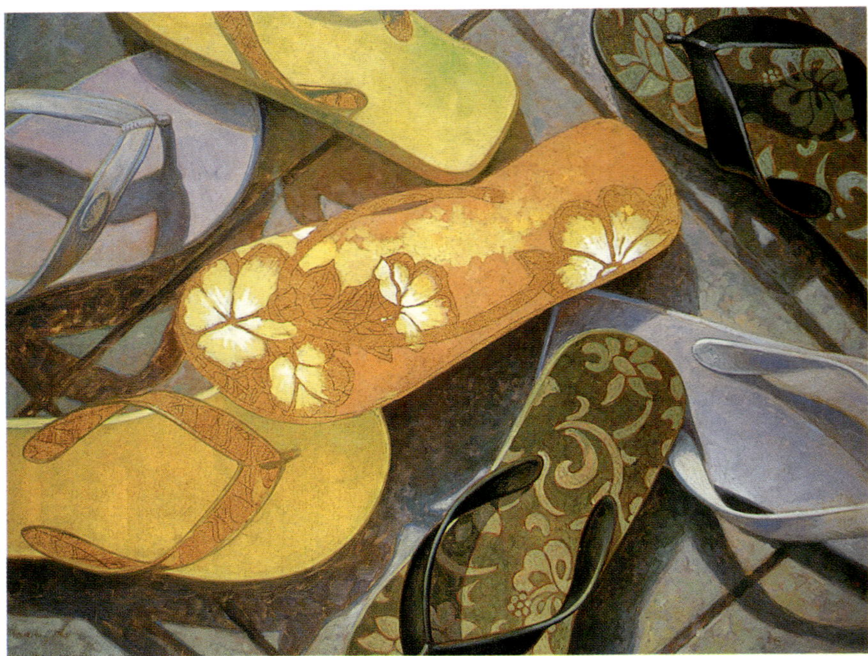

4 Next I paint the base colors of the striped and Hawaiian flower shoes, using mostly yellows and yellow-greens for the striped sandals. I lighten these values with white and darken them with cadmium yellow, yellow ochre, or sap green. Then I use cadmium orange and sap green to paint the yellow soles in shadow. For the Hawaiian pattern, I fill in the white, yellow, and orange background areas, adding cadmium red light to deepen the oranges.

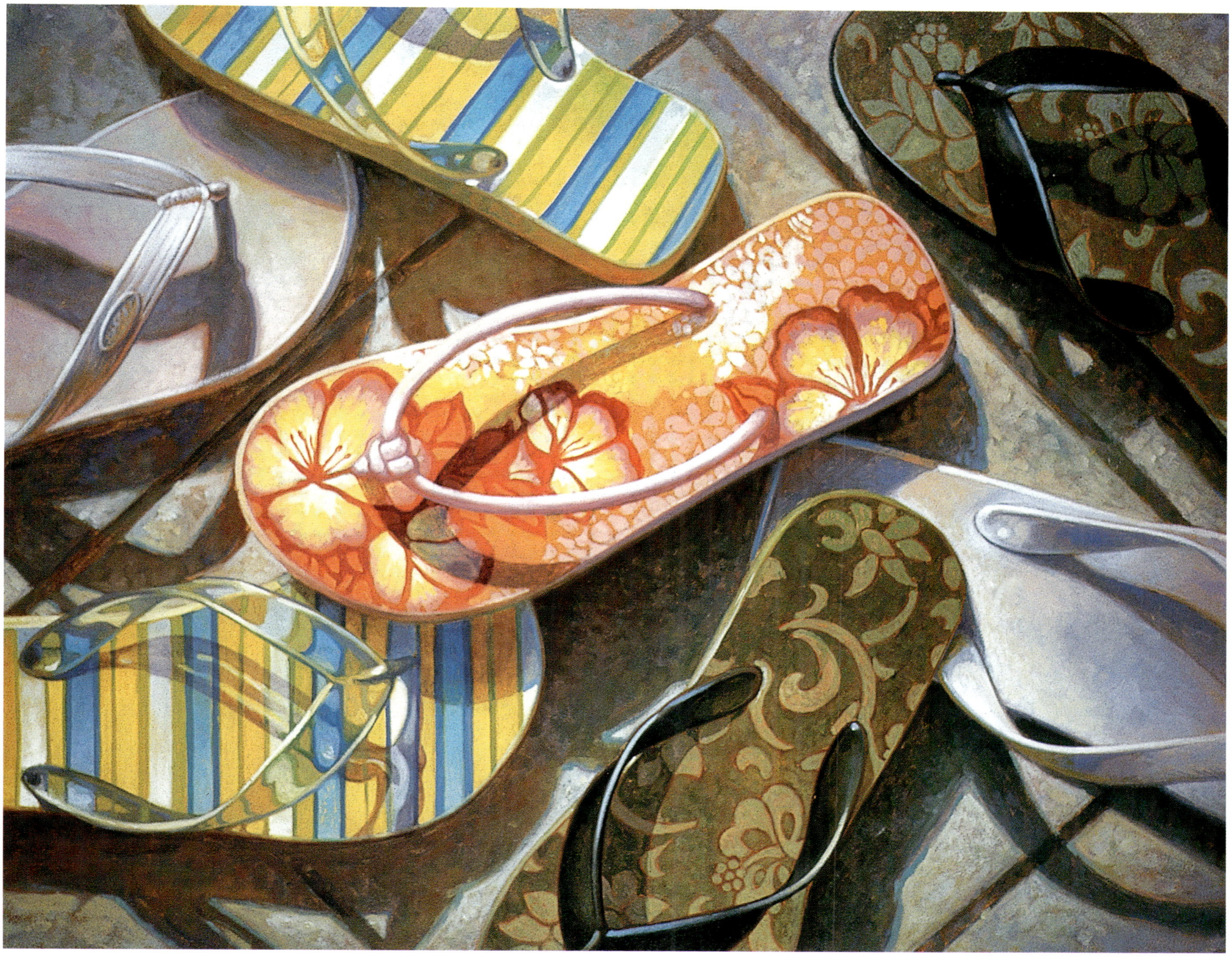

7 I paint over the shadows with a soft brush and transparent glazes of alizarin crimson and dioxazine purple. Next I paint the Hawaiian shoe straps with mixes of alizarin crimson, cadmium red light, and white, darkened with dioxazine purple. For the straps on the striped shoes, I use the same colors as the shoe, only darkened and neutralized with some black. After finishing all the separate colors, I use my detail brush to trace along the edges of the strap and clean up the outline; this is one of the best techniques for making the painting look more realistic. Finally I develop the highlights on the white shoes and on the black straps of the green shoes, and my painting is complete.

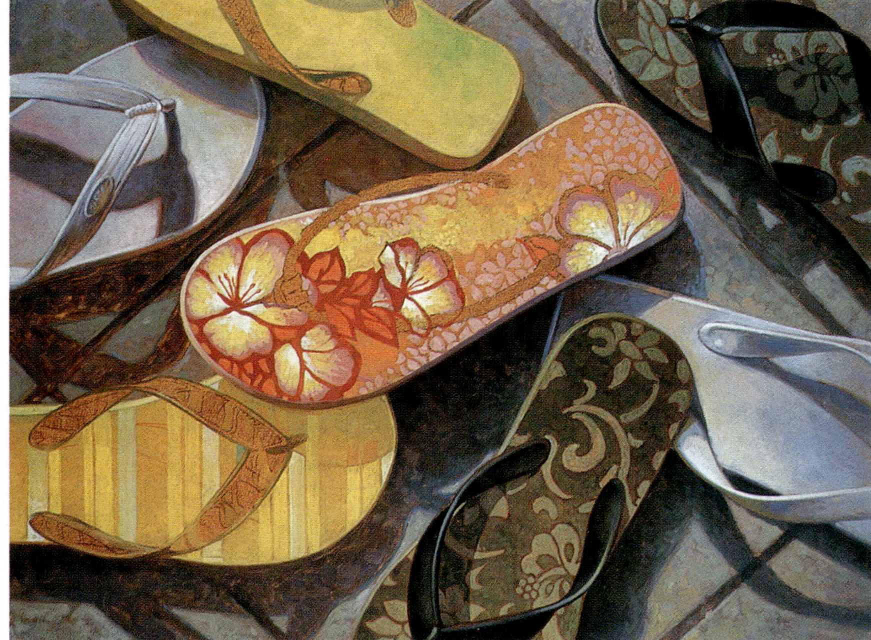

5 Next I paint the small pink flowers with a mix of alizarin crimson, cadmium red light, and white. Toward the back of the shoes and around the outer edges of the largest flowers, I add dioxazine purple to darken and cool the pinks. For the interiors of the leaves, I use alizarin crimson and cadmium orange. Then I use cadmium red light and alizarin crimson for the dark red outline of the large flowers. Next I add reflected color from the surrounding shoes to the white thongs.

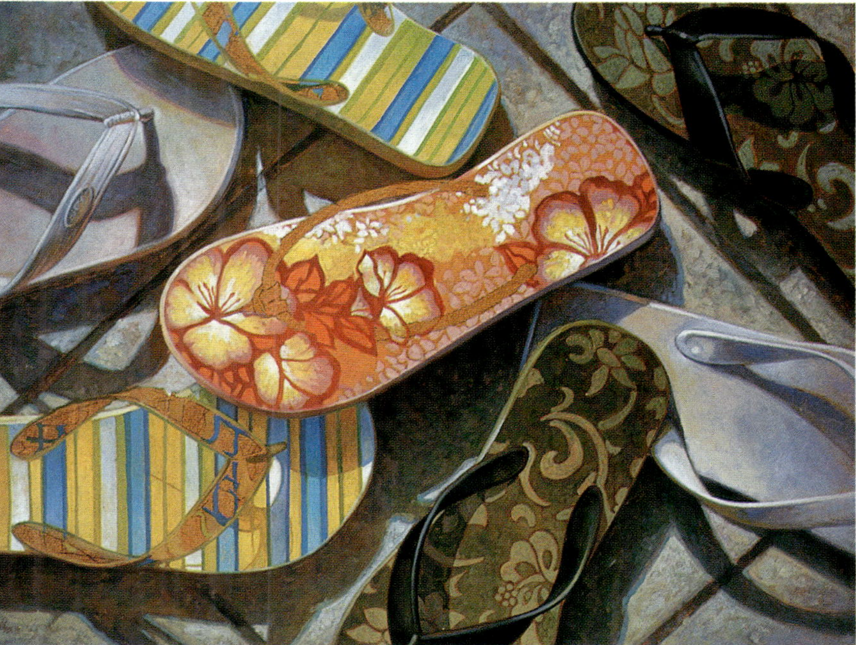

6 Now I paint the wide blue (cerulean blue and white), white, and green (cadmium yellow and sap green) stripes, leaving the base color for the yellow stripes. Then I use white to clean up the edges of the stripes and create a subtle highlight around the edge of the shoes (between the top and the side). I also spend some time lightening and adding texture to the floor around the shoes, where I paint a bluish transition between the shadows and the light.

Toning the Canvas

by Caroline Zimmermann

Many artists begin their paintings with an *underpainting*—a thin layer of color that covers the entire support, eliminating the white of the canvas and providing a base color that will interact with the additional applications of paint. Some choose a hue that's in the same family as the subject, such as a yellow tone for a painting of bananas. Other artists cover the canvas with the complement of the subject in order to subdue the final hues, such as a red base for a group of green trees. Artist Caroline Zimmermann begins most of her paintings with a deep base of reds and oranges, even if the colors aren't present in the subject. The subtle radiance of these hues shows through the top layers of paint and intensifies the final tones, as you can see in this simple grouping of four yellow pears.

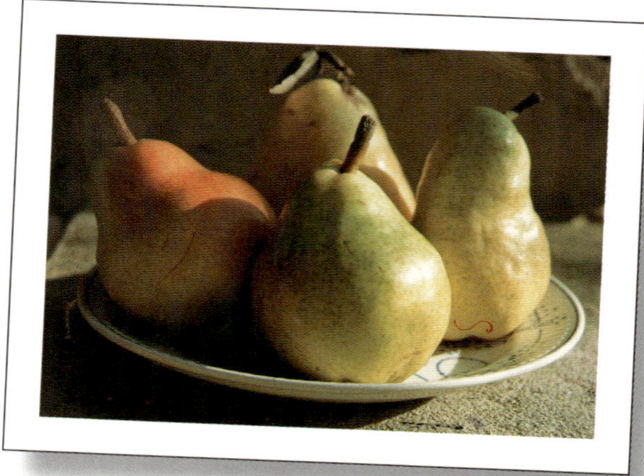

► **STUDYING FORM** Still lifes are wonderful subjects for studying form and shape, and these pears are an excellent example. Their smooth surface and uncomplicated lines allow you to easily observe the way light and shadow work together to help define an object's form.

BUILDING ON THE UNDERPAINTING

Once the underpainting for the pears is established, Caroline works from dark to light, beginning with the darker values of the base color to define the initial shapes and then building up the forms with progressively lighter values and colors. The result is a study in the transition of light to shadow, referred to as "chiaroscuro"; here the richness of the underpainting helps create the dramatic contrasts in light and dark that make this still life so intriguing.

Color Palette

alizarin crimson, cadmium red light, cadmium yellow light, cadmium yellow medium, dioxazine purple, Indian yellow, lemon yellow, sap green, titanium white, transparent orange, ultramarine blue

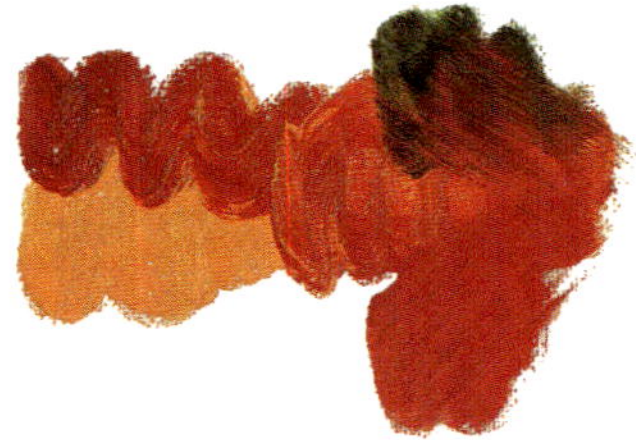

PEAR MID-RANGE VALUES
Cadmium yellow medium + alizarin crimson + cadmium red light + sap green

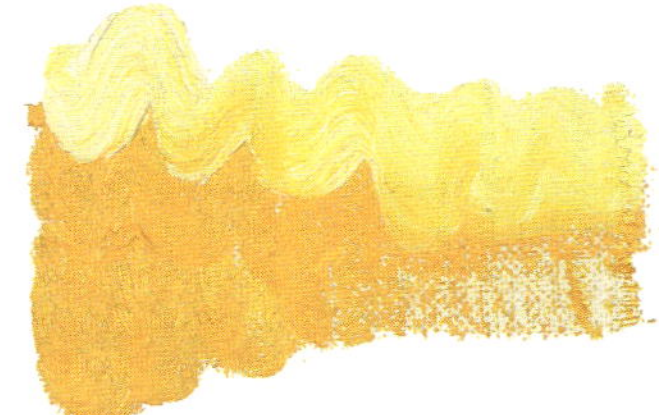

PEAR HIGHLIGHTS
Lemon yellow + cadmium yellow light + white

BACKGROUND
Dioxazine purple + alizarin crimson + ultramarine blue

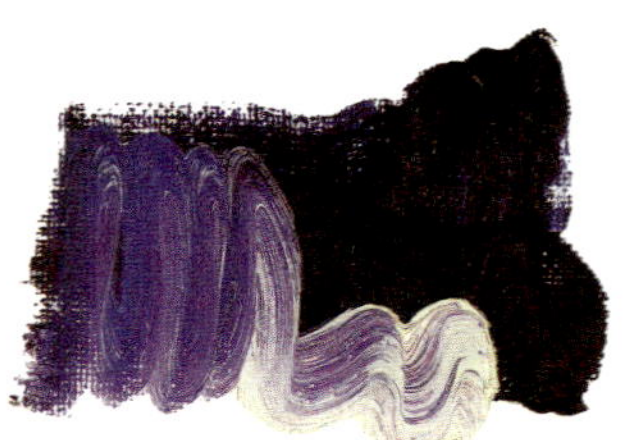

BACKGROUND SHADOWS
Ultramarine blue + dioxazine purple + titanium white

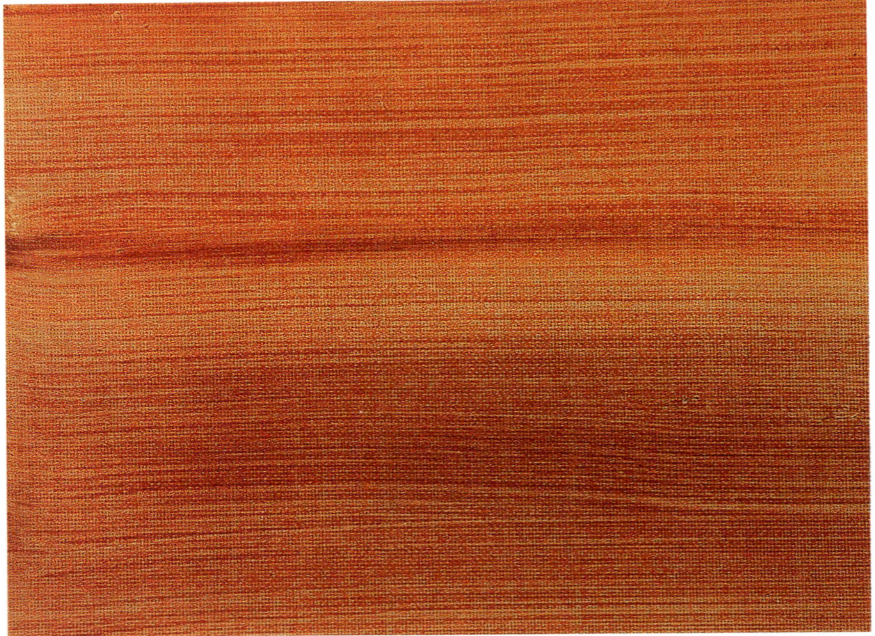

1 I begin with an underpainting of alizarin crimson, Indian yellow, and transparent orange, thinning each pigment with enough solvent to create a fluid, transparent consistency. In a well-ventilated studio and using a large brush, I loosely apply the base color. (I like to think of the underpainting as a warm-up exercise for what is yet to come.) Then I set the canvas outside my studio or away from my workspace to allow the solvent's fumes to evaporate.

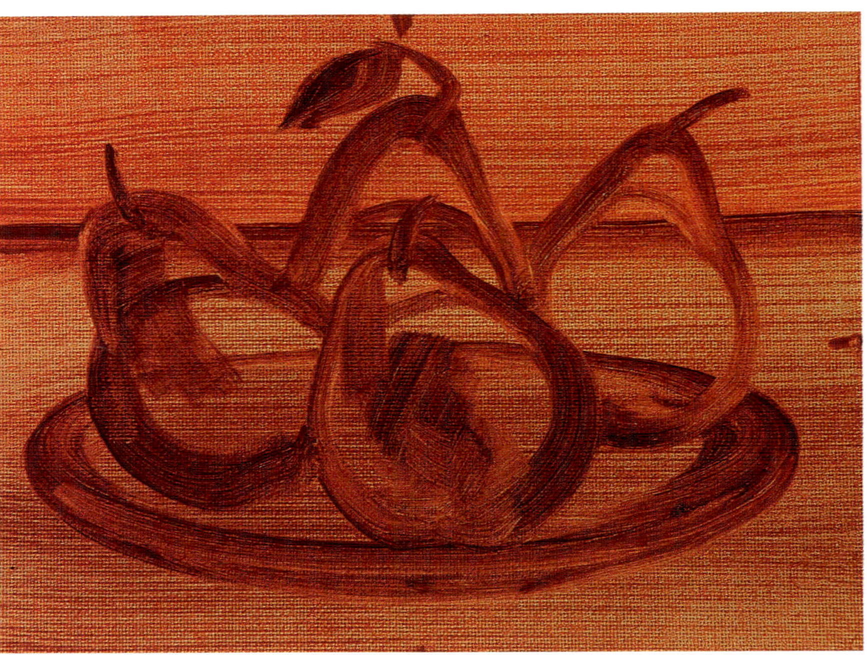

2 I loosely sketch in the composition of my painting with a small bright brush and thinned mixes of alizarin crimson and dioxazine purple. Next I mark the midpoints (vertically) and the center (horizontally) of the composition. Then I draw the "horizon line"—the back of the table—placed slightly off center so I don't visually cut the painting in half. Then I loosely draw the shapes of the fruit in their general locations, keeping their definition to a minimum at this stage.

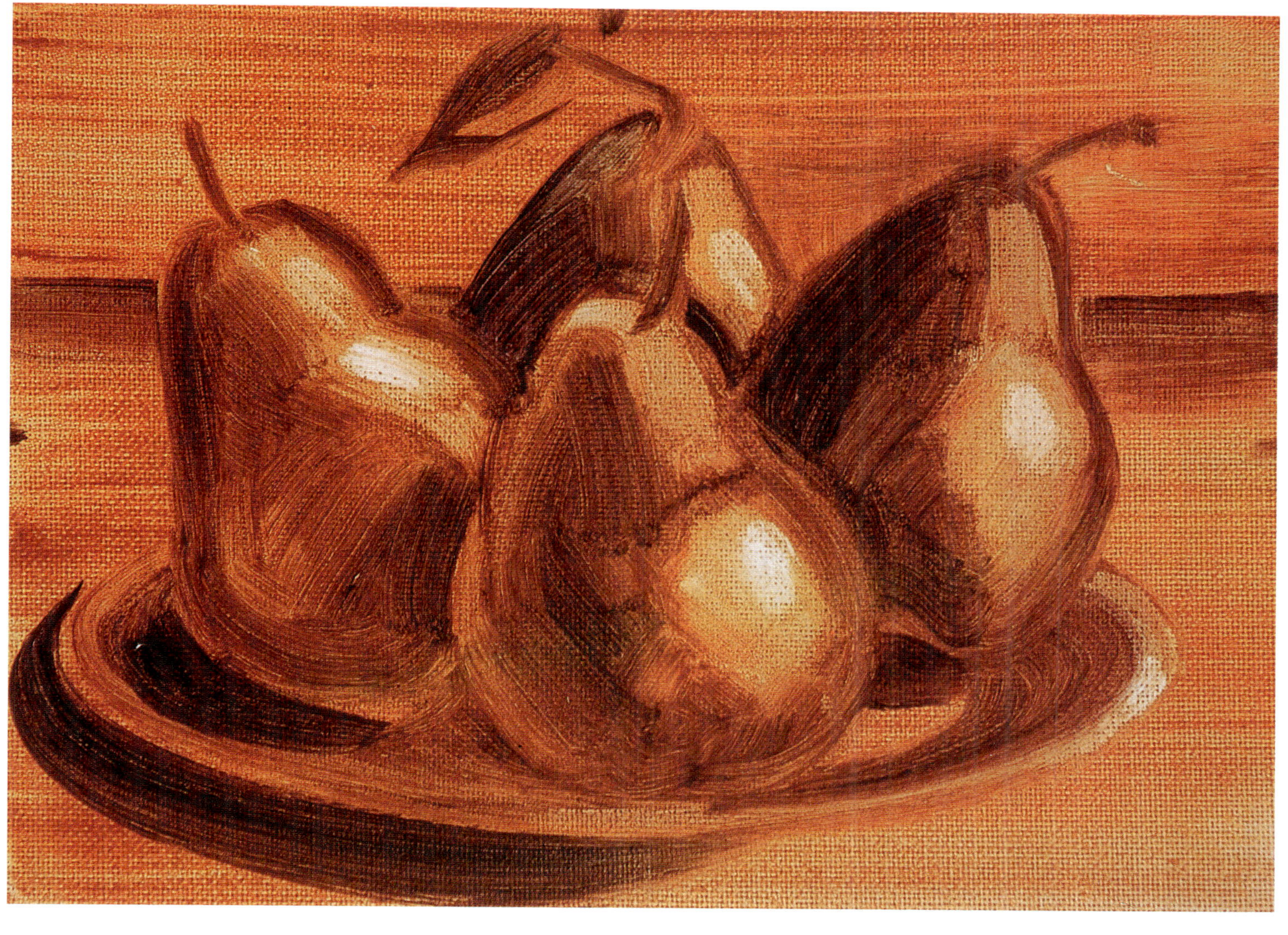

3 Now I draw the objects in more specific detail. With a small flat brush, I use thinned alizarin crimson and dioxazine purple to block in the dark values of the pears, the dish, and the background. Then I indicate the shape of the shadow under the dish and mark where the final highlights will be by removing some paint with a clean brush. For the highlights on the pears, I dab off the color with a clean flannel rag.

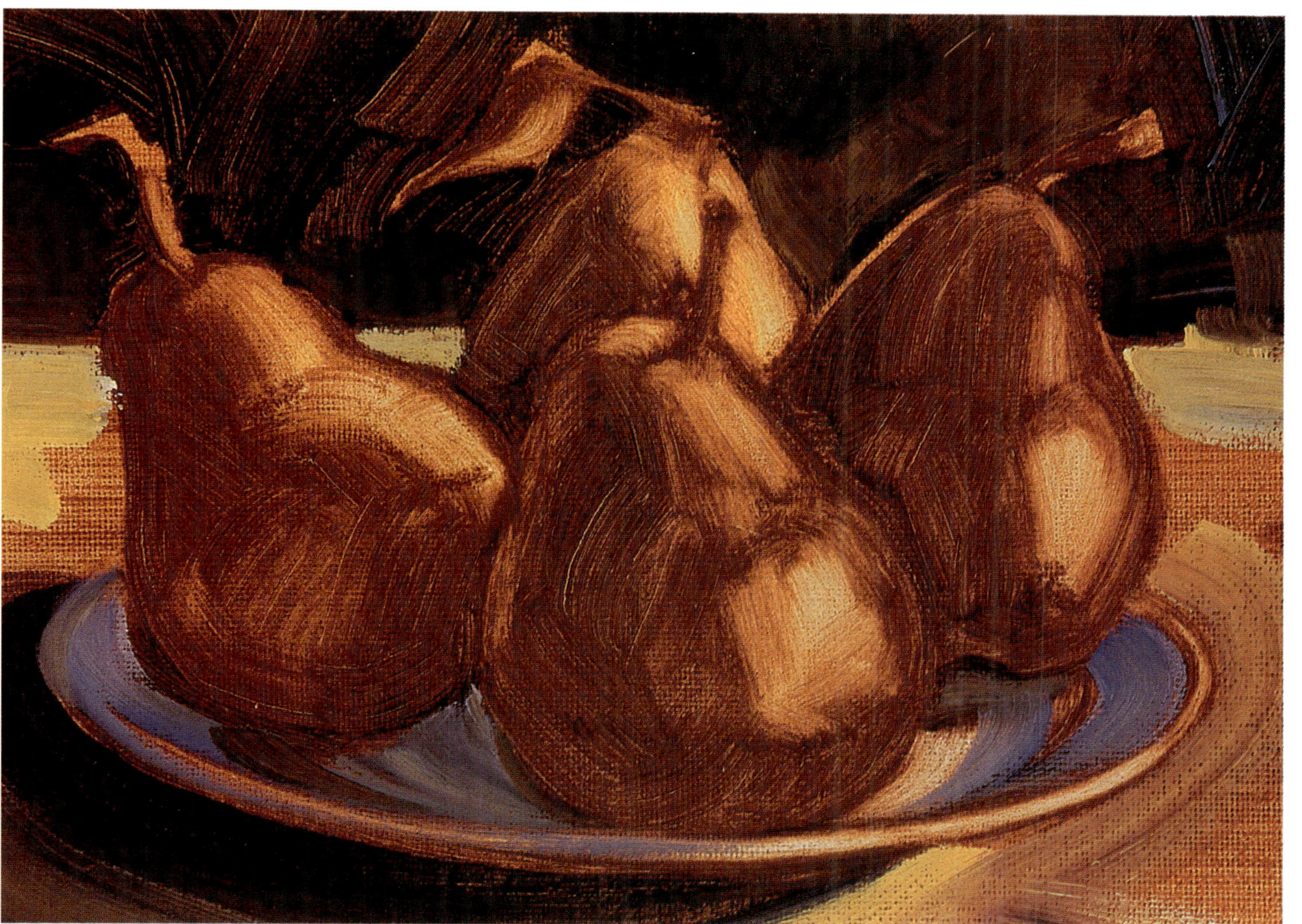

4 I establish the direction of the light source while building up the colors in the background, the shadows, and the foreground. Because colors in shadow are almost never black, I use a mix of ultramarine blue, titanium white, and a touch of dioxazine purple for the darkest values. For other dark areas, I use different variations of ultramarine blue, dioxazine purple, sap green, and alizarin crimson—all transparent pigments that mix together to create rich shades of black. I use a mixture of dioxazine purple, alizarin crimson, and ultramarine blue to begin establishing the dark background. Then I paint the table with a mixture of titanium white and transparent orange, varied with some dioxazine purple for the look of wood grain.

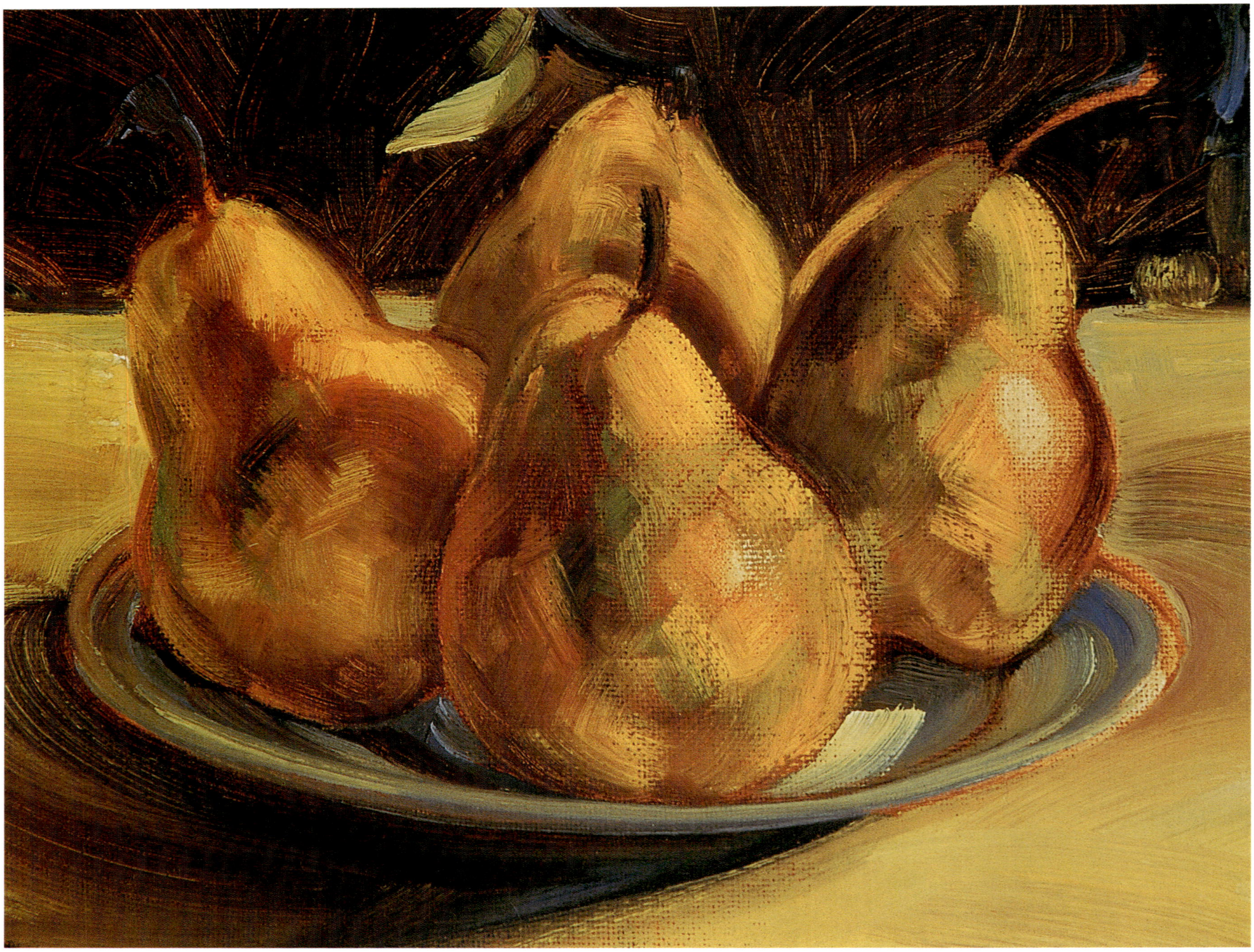

5 I begin the pear shapes with a combination of cadmium yellow medium and alizarin crimson; then I add dabs of cadmium red light and sap green for the shadow areas. While the paint is still wet, I blend in some cadmium yellow light to begin the dark-to-light transition on the pears. For the purple shadows on the white plate, I use white mixed with ultramarine blue and dioxazine purple. For the leaf on the middle pear, I mix sap green and lemon yellow; for the stems, I use a combination of dioxazine purple and ultramarine blue.

► PEAR DETAIL STEP ONE
I start by painting the basic shapes that constitute each pear: a set of irregular circles. Although each pear has the same general shape, I look for unique characteristics and make each pear slightly different.

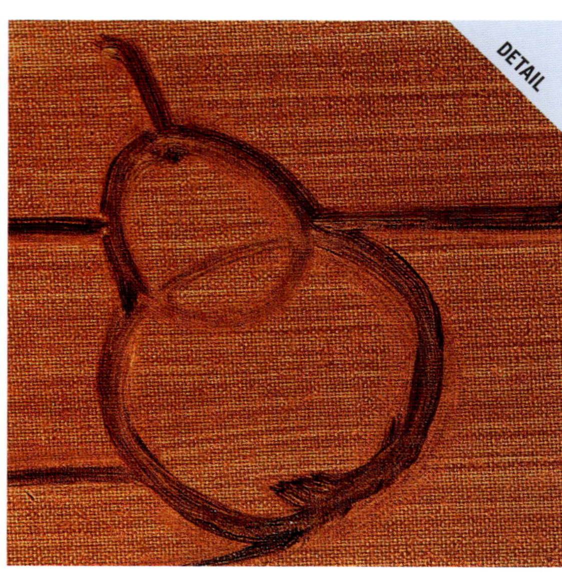

► PEAR DETAIL STEP TWO
As I begin to add the details and highlights to the pears, I frequently consult my reference photo, noting the direction of the light source and observing the shapes of the shadows.

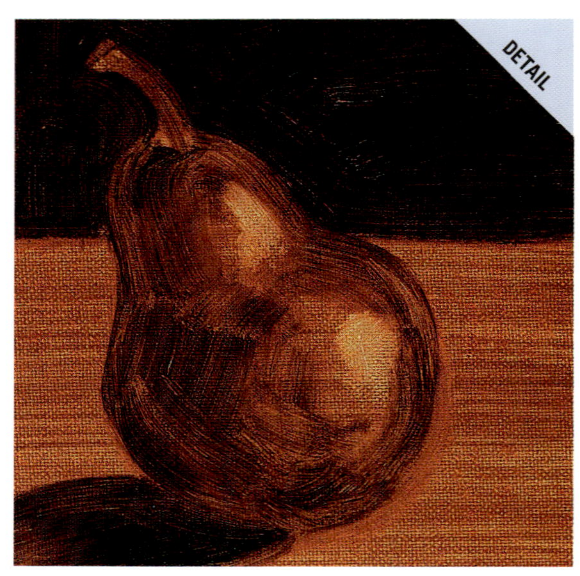

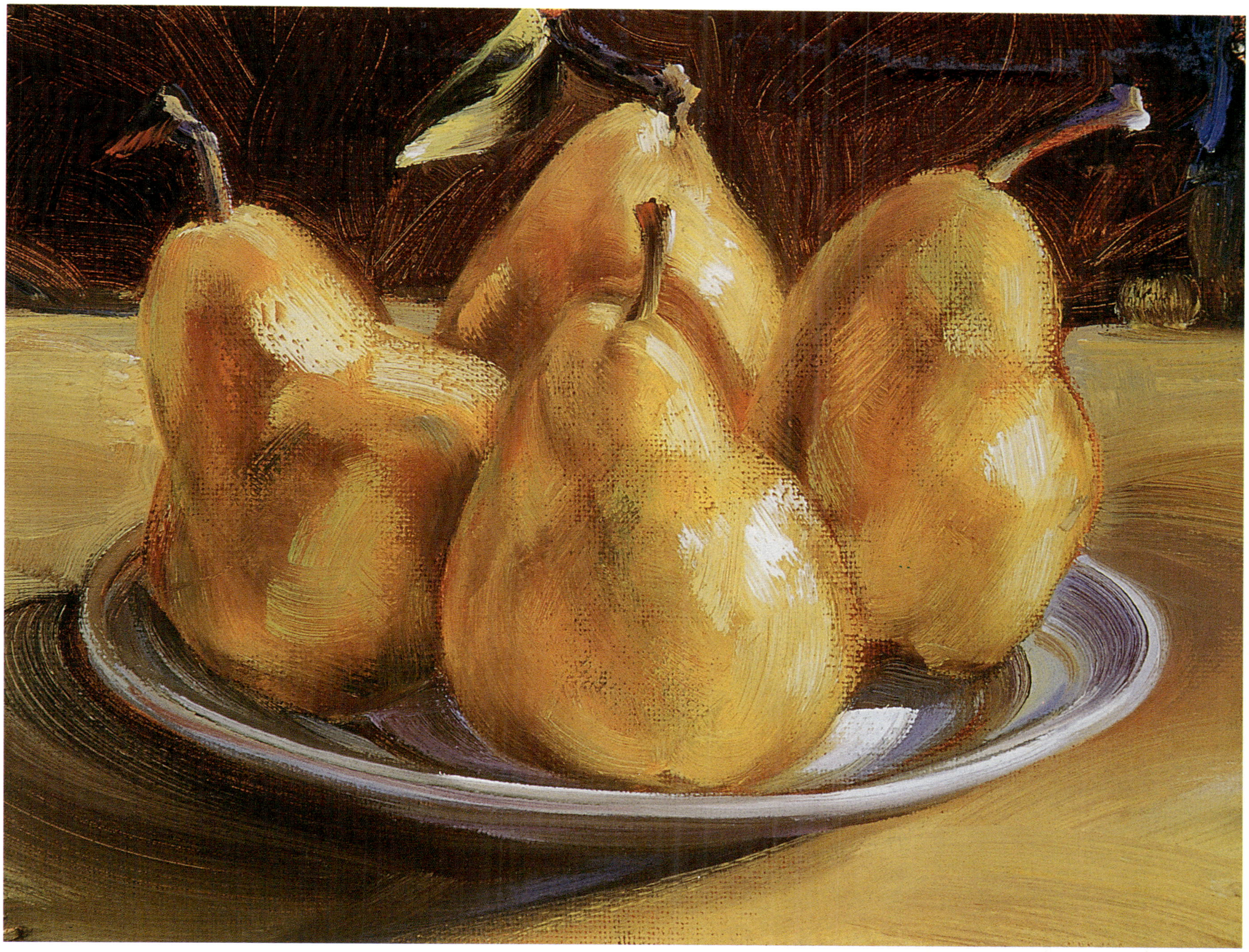

6 To apply the final highlights, I use a medium flat brush and quick, light strokes that don't disturb the underlying colors. For the highlight on the pears, I use a mixture of lemon yellow, titanium white, and cadmium yellow medium, adding a touch of white on the stems for dimension. I accent the leaf with lemon yellow mixed with titanium white, reserving pure titanium white for only the last and final touches—one highlight on each pear and a stroke on the plate for a reflective sheen.

► **PEAR DETAIL STEP THREE** As I continue to develop the pears' values, I always keep in mind their *core* colors—the true color of the pears when they are not in bright light or deep shadow. Staying true to the core colors helps me retain the correct relationship between all the values.

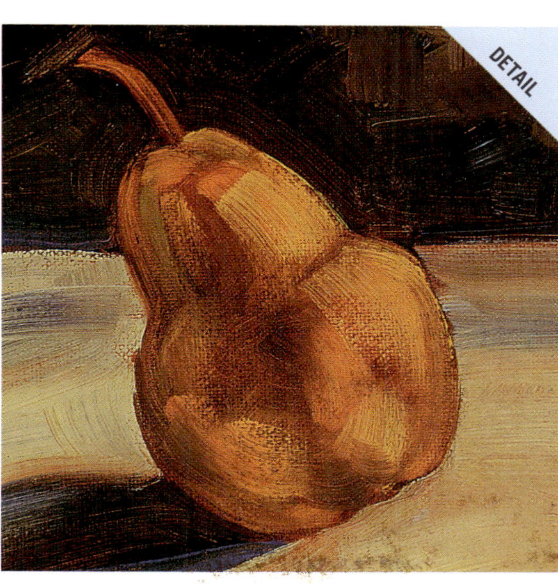

► **PEAR DETAIL STEP FOUR** I always paint the highlights last. These finishing touches are what give the pears their optimum depth and form, as well as their bright, shiny skins.

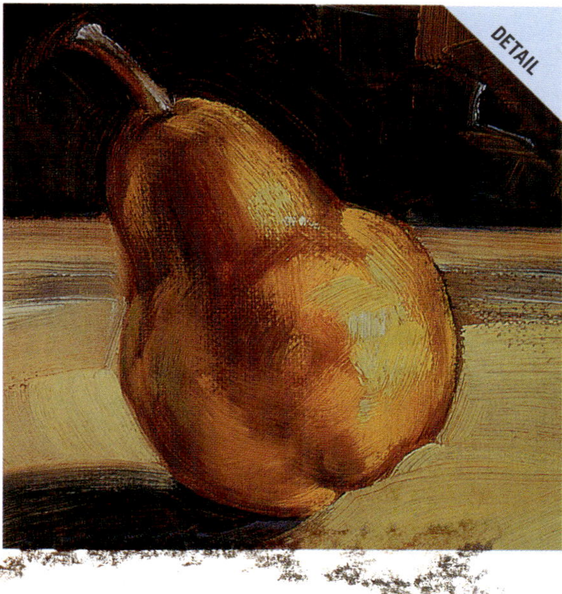

Narrowing the Focus

by Caroline Zimmermann

The center of interest is always an integral part of a still life painting. It's intended to be the main focal point, but it's also just one aspect of the entire arrangement. But sometimes artists do more than make one object a central aspect of a painting; they make it the *only* element in the composition. For this still life, Caroline Zimmermann cropped a photograph containing multiple flowers to "zoom in" on a single, beautiful sunflower. By removing the extraneous elements in the photo and eliminating most of the distracting background, the viewer's attention is directed specifically to the interesting shapes and colors of the flower. And the sharp contrast between the cool, dark colors of the leaves and underlying shadows and the brightness of the golden petals sets off the sunflower even more, making it really stand out and demand to be seen!

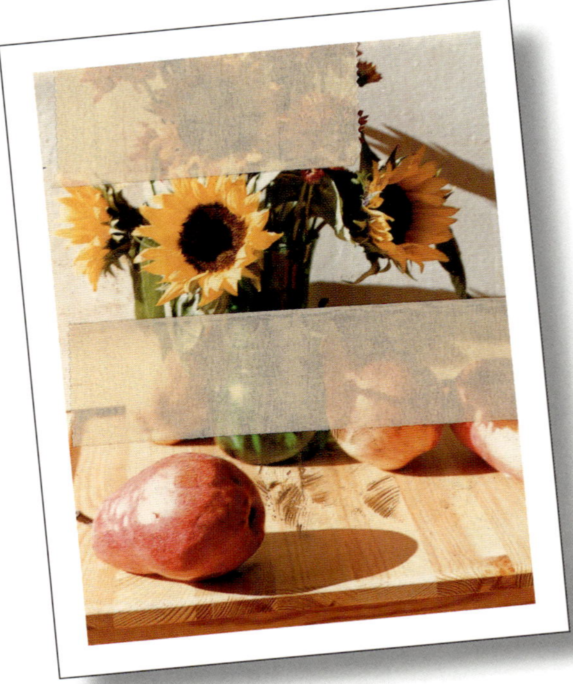

◄ **FINDING THE FOCUS** I started out with a photograph containing multiple flowers in a vase and other background objects. Then I placed removable tape on the photo to act as a viewfinder, framing one spot at a time until I find just the right composition.

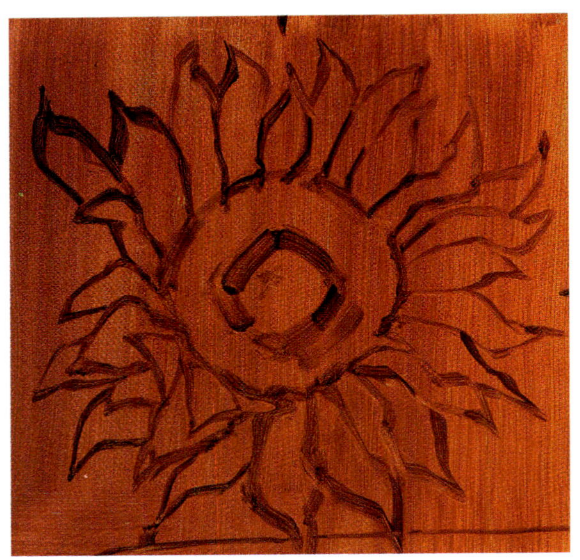

1 I apply a wash of alizarin crimson, Indian yellow, transparent orange, and magenta to create a warm base of color. After the base coat is dry, I loosely draw the sunflower with thinned mixes of alizarin crimson and dioxazine purple, beginning with the center and moving outward to the petals.

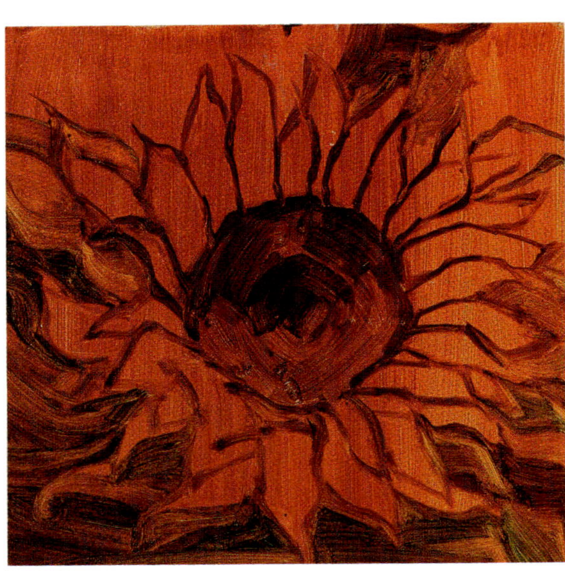

2 Once I am satisfied with the general sketch, I begin to draw the sunflower in more specific detail. With a medium flat brush, I plot out the dark and light areas of the flower's center and the surrounding leaves with mixes of thinned alizarin crimson, dioxazine purple, and sap green.

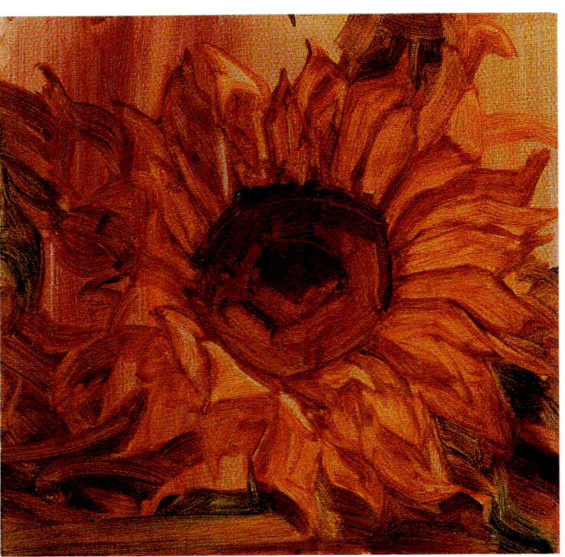

3 With a small flat brush, I add more detail to the petals and leaves with thinned mixes of alizarin crimson, sap green, and magenta. While the oil is still wet, I lift out some paint with a clean brush to indicate where the highlights will eventually be.

Color Palette

alizarin crimson, cadmium red light, cadmium yellow light, cadmium yellow medium, dioxazine purple, Indian yellow, lemon yellow, magenta, permanent rose, sap green, titanium white, transparent orange

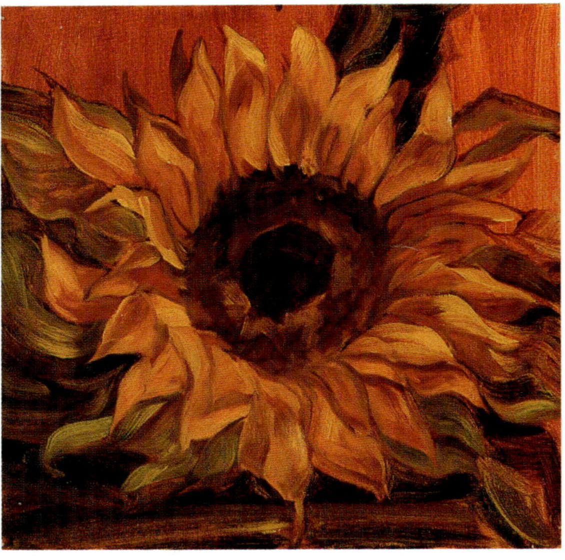

4 I paint the petals with mixes of titanium white, various yellows and reds, transparent orange, and dioxazine purple. For the leaves, I use sap green, alizarin crimson, and cadmium yellow light. For the flower's center, I mix dioxazine purple and alizarin crimson, adding cadmium yellow medium for texture.

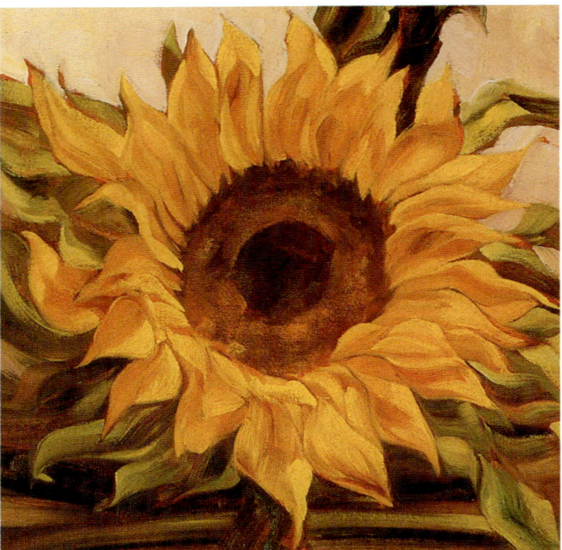

5 After the paint has dried, I brush in the background with a mix of white, magenta, and lemon yellow. I also add cadmium yellow light, transparent orange, and magenta to the petals and sap green and lemon yellow to the leaves. Then I create the center texture with a mix of dioxazine purple and lemon yellow.

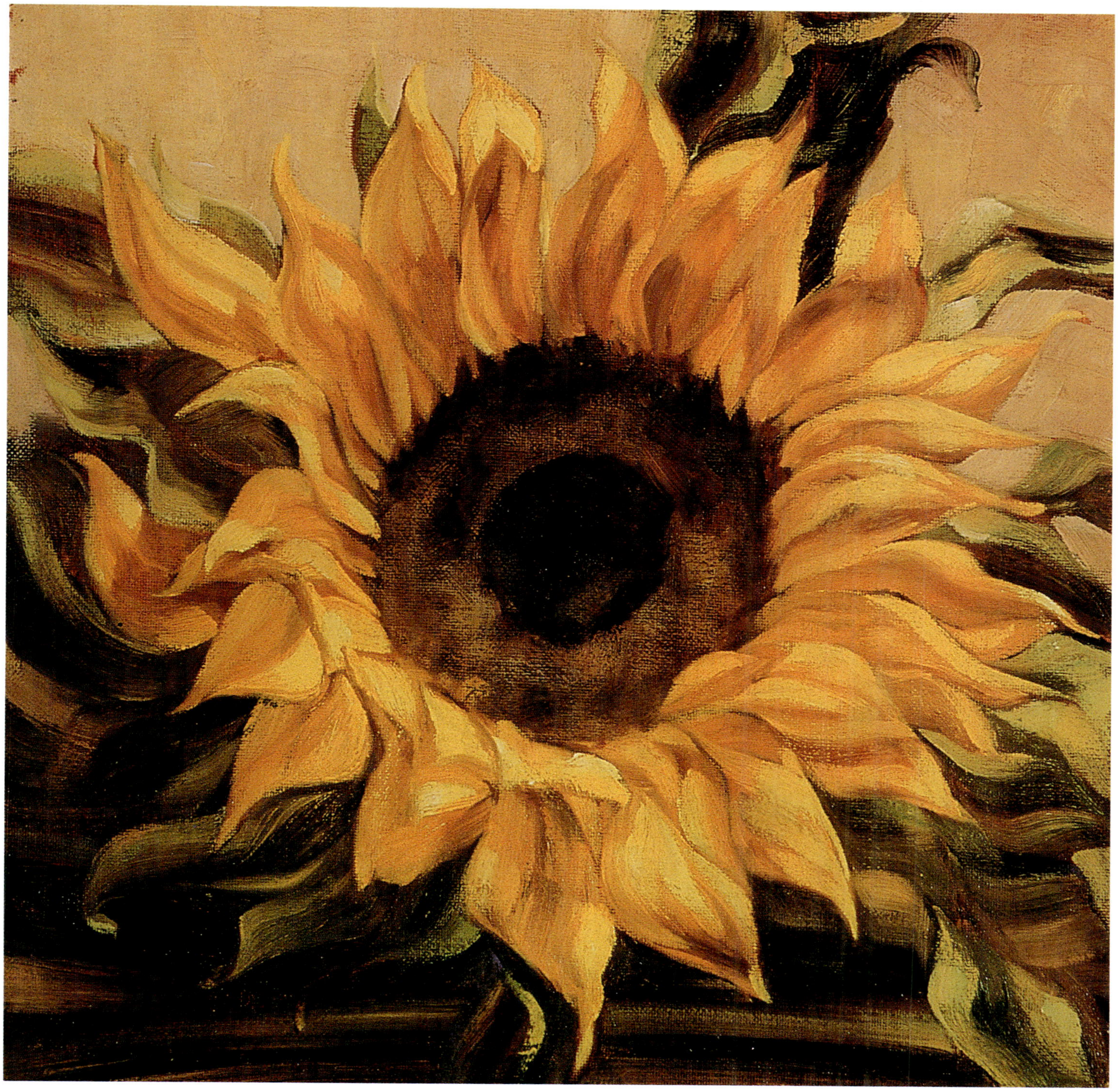

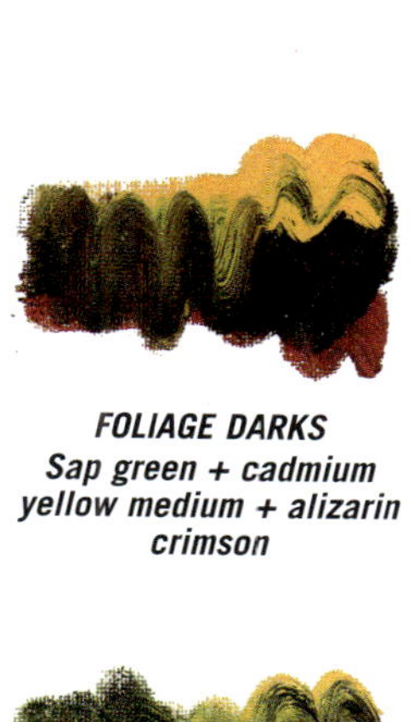

FOLIAGE DARKS
Sap green + cadmium yellow medium + alizarin crimson

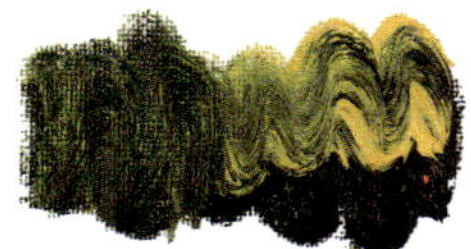

FOLIAGE MID-RANGE VALUES
Sap green + lemon yellow

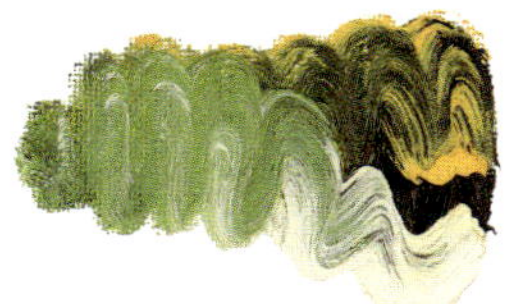

FOLIAGE HIGHLIGHTS
Sap green + lemon yellow + white

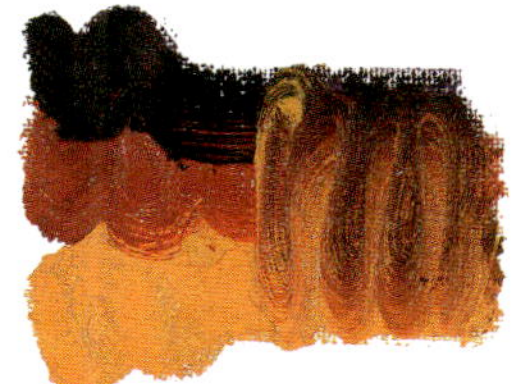

PETAL DARKS
Cadmium yellow medium + transparent orange + dioxazine purple

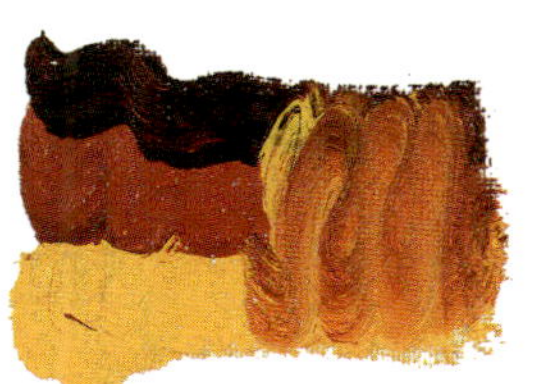

PETAL MID-RANGE VALUES
Cadmium yellow light + transparent orange + magenta

6 Now I'm ready to add my lightest and brightest colors. These final highlights will add more contrast to the dark background, emphasizing my focal point. I first add highlights to the extended petals with a mixture of cadmium yellow light, lemon yellow, and titanium white. Then, to create more dimension in the leaves, I paint the sunlit detail with a combination of sap green, lemon yellow, and titanium white. Finally I revisit the center of the sunflower, refining the texture with gentle touches of dioxazine purple, lemon yellow, and a dab of white. My painting is complete when I'm comfortable with the attention the light and detail of the center receives against the dark and uncomplicated background.

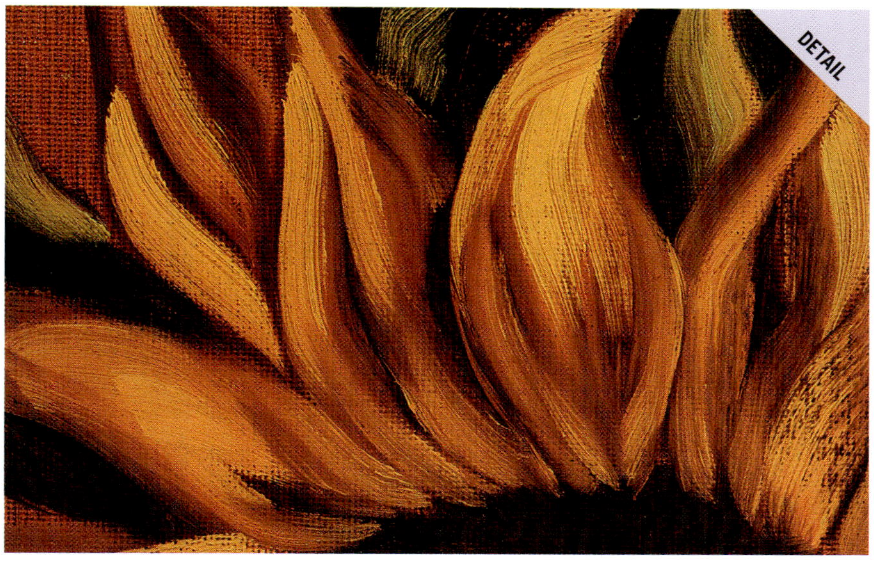

DETAIL

PETALS DETAIL STEP ONE I try to think of the sunflower as a whole shape first, visualizing how it fits into a square format before I begin to draw it in small sections. I study the petals' variations and carefully draw each shape. After I finish painting the lights and darks in the center of the flower, I develop the darker areas and shadows in each of the petals. Notice how the depth and form of the flower really begin to be defined in this step.

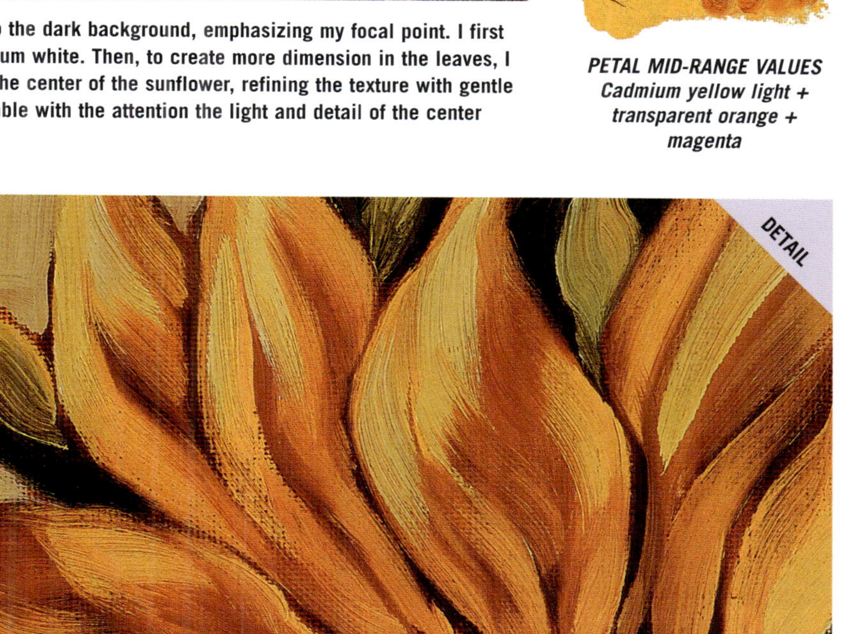

DETAIL

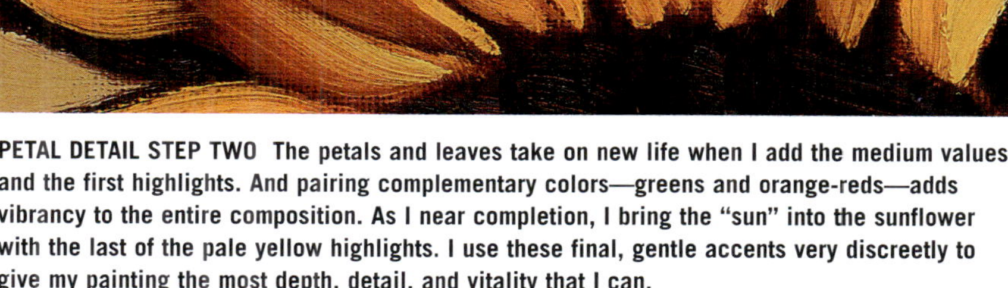

PETAL DETAIL STEP TWO The petals and leaves take on new life when I add the medium values and the first highlights. And pairing complementary colors—greens and orange-reds—adds vibrancy to the entire composition. As I near completion, I bring the "sun" into the sunflower with the last of the pale yellow highlights. I use these final, gentle accents very discreetly to give my painting the most depth, detail, and vitality that I can.

Applying Perspective

by Caroline Zimmermann

Still lifes are meant to create an illusion, fooling the eye into believing that the objects in a painting are real. And one of the most successful ways to make your still life paintings appear realistic is to use the visual cues of *perspective*—the representation of objects in three-dimensional space to create the illusion of depth and distance. One important rule of perspective is that closer objects appear larger and than those in the distance, whether the setting is a vast landscape or an intimate room. For example, in Caroline's painting of a martini setup, the glass is larger than the shaker, even though in reality the opposite is true. And overlapping the two also helps indicate that that the shaker is farther away. Another rule of perspective applies to round or cylindrical objects; when viewed from an angle, they are made up of a series of ellipses rather than circles, as you can see in the shapes of the martini glass and shaker. Keeping these ellipses consistent is key to making these objects appear as realistic as possible. So observe your reference carefully and faithfully mimic the shapes and proportions you see. The better the initial drawing is, the easier and more fun the later stages of the painting will be!

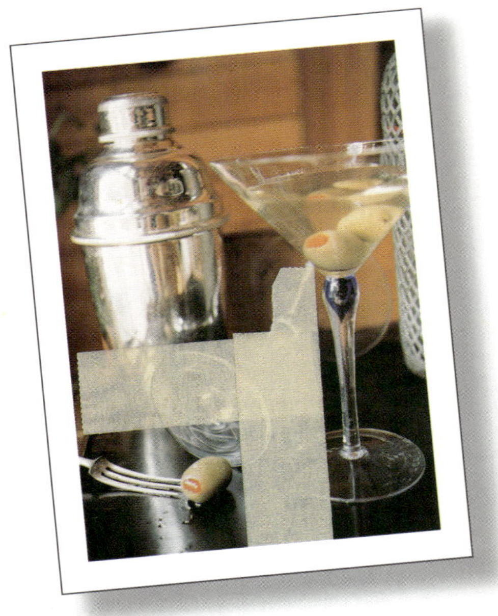

▲ **FOCUSING ON THE ELEMENTS** A complicated-looking setup like this one is easy to approach when you look at it as pieces rather than as a whole. I use artist's tape to break up the composition into individual elements before I begin sketching.

Color Palette

alizarin crimson, cadmium red medium, cadmium yellow medium, dioxazine purple, Indian yellow, lemon yellow, magenta, sap green, titanium white, transparent orange, ultramarine blue

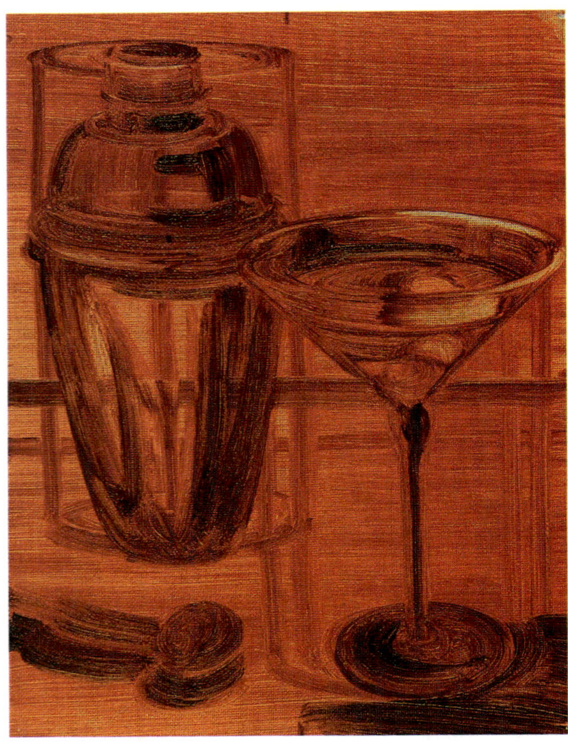

1 I begin the painting with thin washes of Indian yellow, transparent orange, and magenta. Then, once the paint is dry, I loosely sketch the composition with a medium flat brush and a mix of alizarin crimson and dioxazine purple. I block in the basic shapes, sketching the martini glass and the shaker inside two cylinders to help define their forms. Then I begin to draw the objects in more detail; with a medium flat brush, I apply alizarin crimson mixed with solvent to plot out the forms of the glass and the reflective patterns on the shaker. It's important to establish the correct perspective right away.

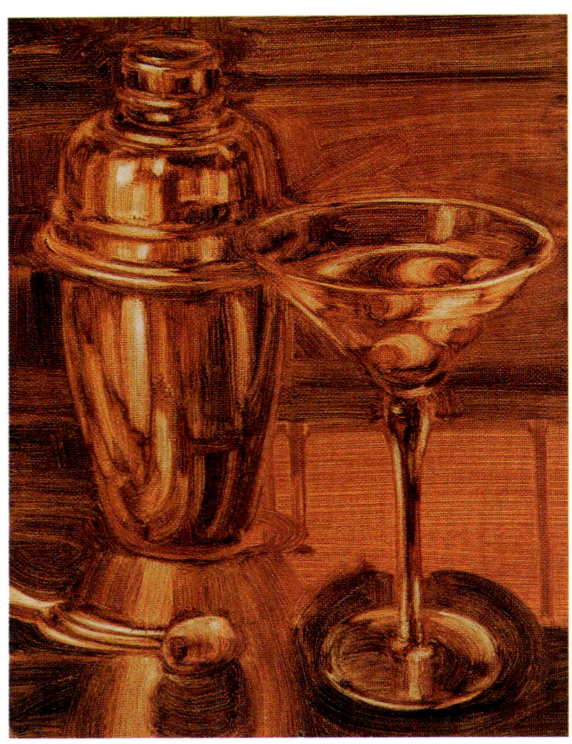

2 Next I use a small flat brush and a mix of alizarin crimson, sap green, and magenta to add more detail to the scene. While the color is still wet, I paint in a "reductive" manner: I clean my brush with solvent, blot it on a rag, and lift away paint where the highlights will be. (This technique utilizes the white of the canvas to indicate the highlights rather than relying on white paint.) The highlights are an important part of accurately rendering the metal shaker; the light shapes contrast with the dark shapes to visually convey the fact that the surface is reflective.

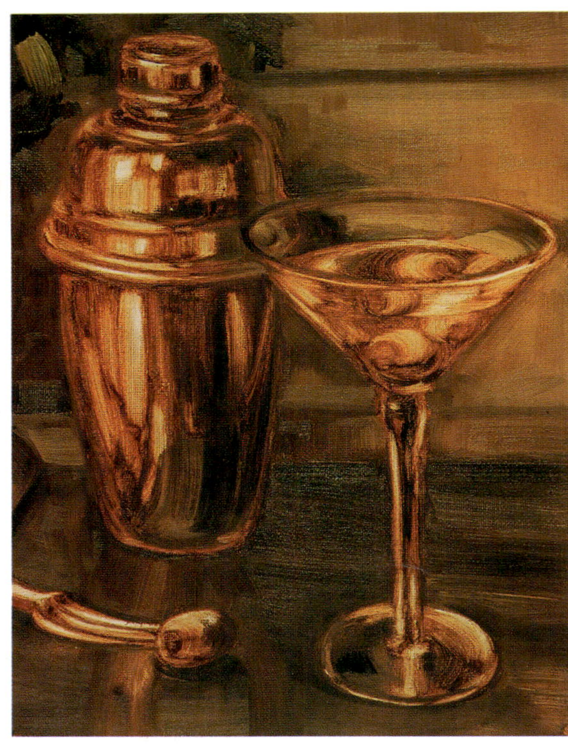

3 Now I work from dark to light to build a rich reflective surface. First I create a semblance of foliage behind the shaker with mixtures of sap green and alizarin crimson. Then I add small amounts of cadmium yellow medium to mixtures of alizarin crimson, sap green, and ultramarine blue to create the wood surfaces, adding a little more cadmium yellow medium for the panel in the background. For the dark areas of the silver and the glass, I use mixes of sap green, ultramarine blue, and alizarin crimson. I also block in the olives. (See details on page 29.)

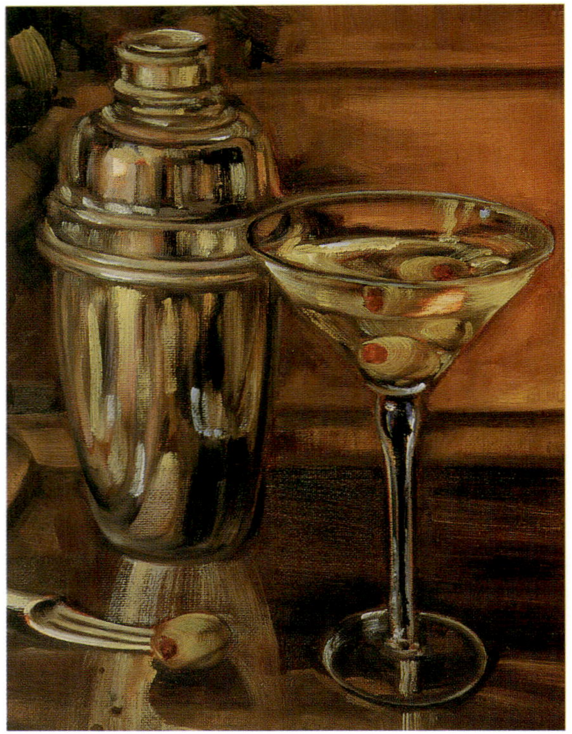

4 There are many variations in the grays of this scene; I use mixtures of complementary colors that are already on my palette, always adding a touch of white to create a muted tone. I mix the warm grays with lemon yellow and dioxazine purple, and I use a mix of ultramarine blue and transparent orange for the cool grays. I also use touches of cadmium yellow medium and white to form highlights; then I build up the middle tones in the olives and paint reflections in the glass. When painting glass and metal, keep in mind that you're actually painting just the shadows and reflections of light.

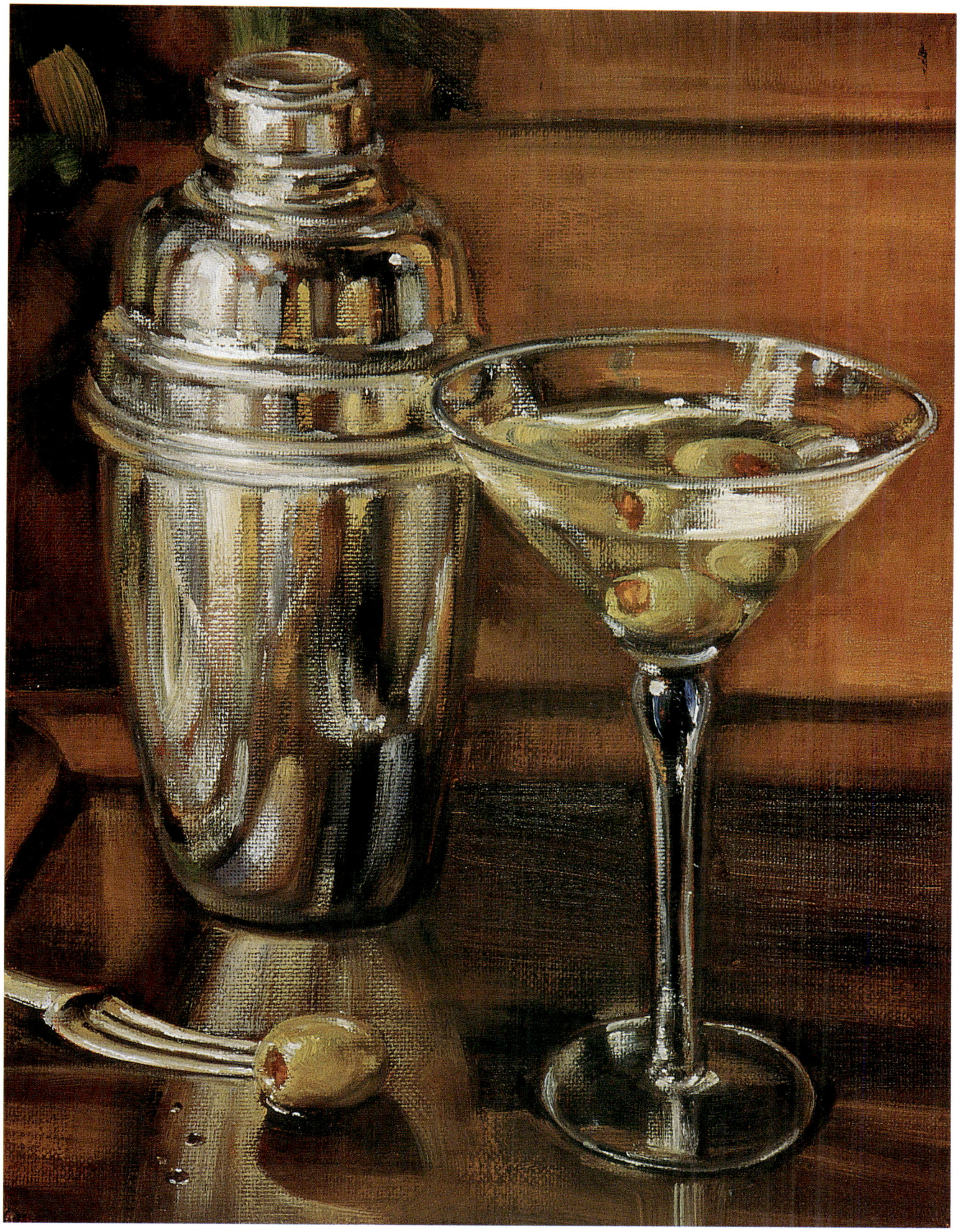

5 Now I put some sparkle on the reflective surfaces and bring out the highlights. But to maintain the optical illusion of depth and reflection, I pay close attention to the darkest shapes. I apply the lightest values (white mixed with touches of the gray tones from step four) to the reflections on the shaker, the fork, and the liquid in the glass. Then, to create the thin white highlights, I drag the edge of a medium flat brush perpendicularly across the painting surface. Finally I add the final highlights to the olives, and the painting is complete—cheers!

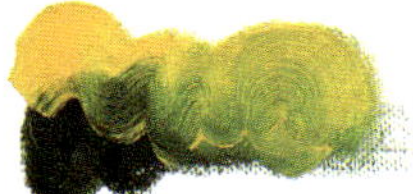

OLIVE HIGHLIGHTS
Sap green + lemon yellow

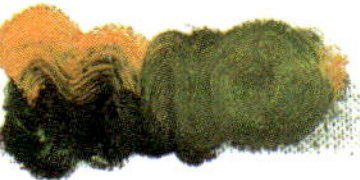

OLIVE MID-RANGE
Sap green + cad. yellow med.

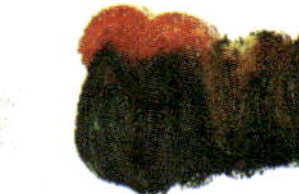

OLIVE DARKS
Sap green + transparent orange

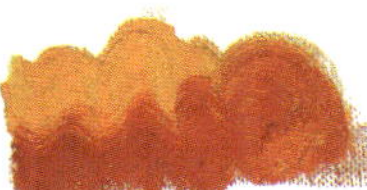

PIMENTO HIGHLIGHTS
Cad. red med. + cad. yellow med.

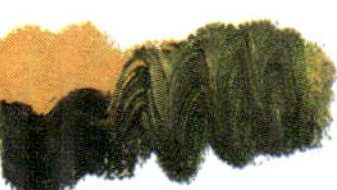

WOOD MID-RANGE
Sap green + cad. yellow med.

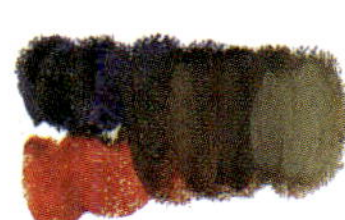

BACKGROUND FOLIAGE MID-RANGE
Ultra. blue + trans. orange + white

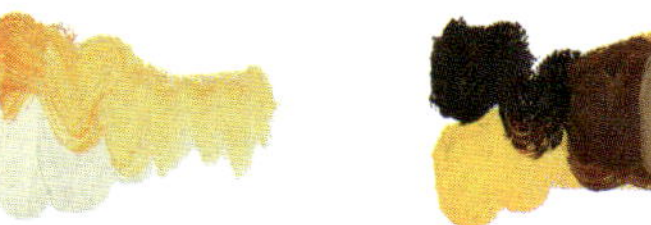

SILVER HIGHLIGHTS
White + cad. yellow med.

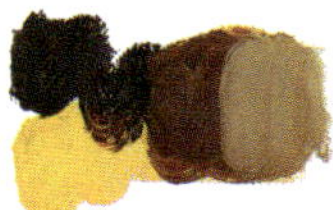

SILVER MID-RANGE
Dioxazine purple + lemon yellow + white

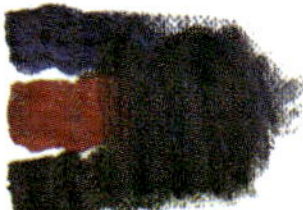

SILVER DARKS
Sap green + alizarin crimson + ultramarine blue

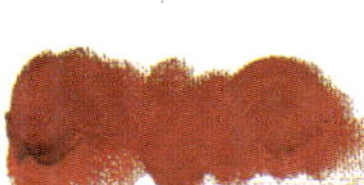

PIMENTO DARKS
Cad. red med. + alizarin crimson

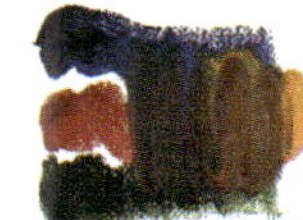

WOOD DARKS
Sap green + alizarin crimson + ultra. blue + cad. yellow med.

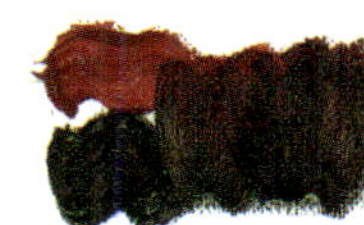

BACKGROUND FOLIAGE DARKS
Sap green + alizarin crimson

Painting the Olives

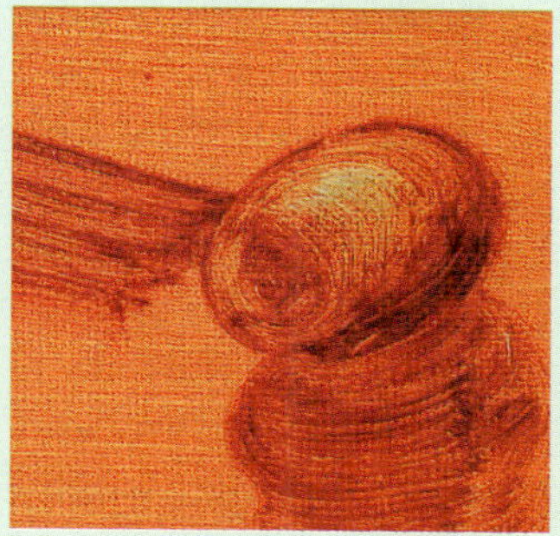

I loosely sketch each olive (shown is the one with the fork) with alizarin crimson thinned with solvent.

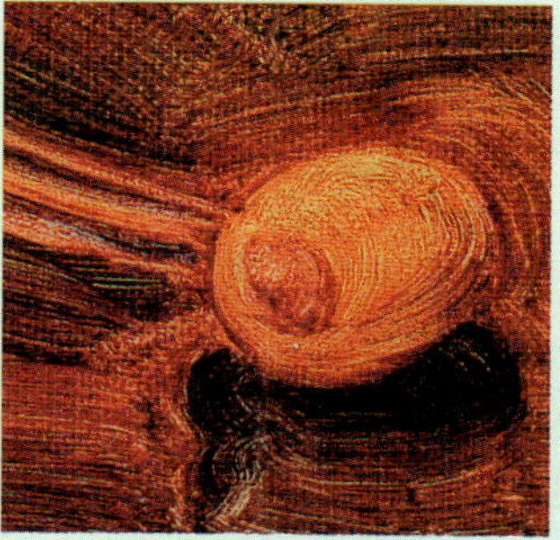

Next I block in the darks of the olives using a deep green mix of sap green and transparent orange.

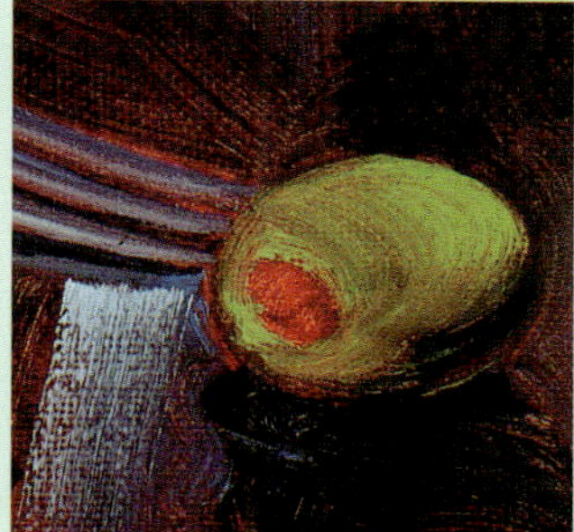

Then I apply mixes of sap green and cadmium yellow medium to the light areas of the olives, using cadmium red medium and alizarin crimson for the pimentos.

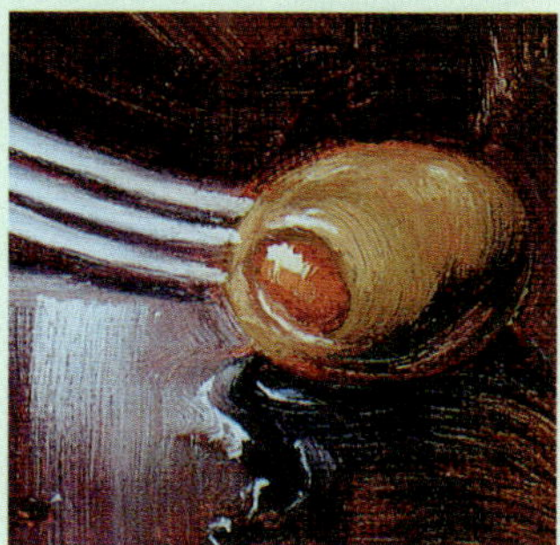

I use a mix of sap green and lemon yellow for the highlights, and then I add a final touch of white. I add the pimento highlights with a mix of cadmium red medium and cadmium yellow medium.

Painting Floral Bouquets

by Caroline Zimmermann

Flowers are incredibly colorful and lively subjects that are wonderful subjects for an oil painting. When setting up a floral still life, it's helpful to follow some simple guidelines that will give your arrangement movement and interest. Start by using a variety of shapes, sizes, and colors. Try not to overcrowd the flowers in the vase; let them droop and sprawl at varying angles, as they are in this painting. These varying lines and angles will give the viewer's eye a path to follow and will keep the composition from seeming stagnant. And choose a simple container that won't overpower the flowers; you want them to be the focal point. Here Caroline Zimmermann creates a pleasing floral composition with repetition of diagonals, varying textures, and contrasts of light against dark for added visual interest. The long, dark shadows and single rose lying on the table act as visual paths that draw your eye into the scene and then up to the crystal vase of beautiful red roses.

Color Palette

alizarin crimson, cadmium red light, cadmium red medium, cadmium yellow light, cadmium yellow medium, dioxazine purple, Indian yellow, lemon yellow, magenta, permanent rose, sap green, titanium white, transparent orange, ultramarine blue

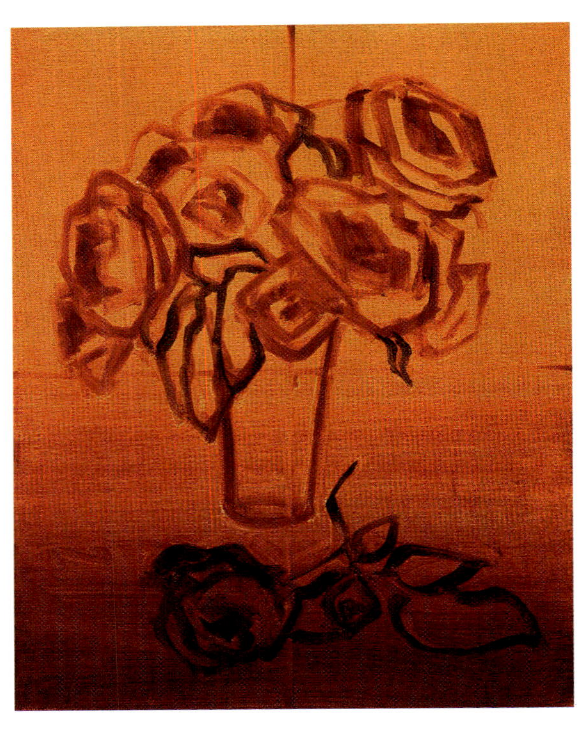

1 I begin with a transparent underpainting of alizarin crimson, Indian yellow, and transparent orange, thinning each pigment with solvent. I gradually the colors from yellow on the top (where it will be easy to see the drawing and the dark areas), working down to the orange and alizarin crimson foreground for the table. Then I loosely establish the drawing with a thinned mixture of alizarin crimson and dioxazine purple, indicating the horizontal and vertical midpoints with perpendicular guidelines. As I draw, I vary the shapes of the individual flowers, keeping in mind the outer shape of the entire bouquet.

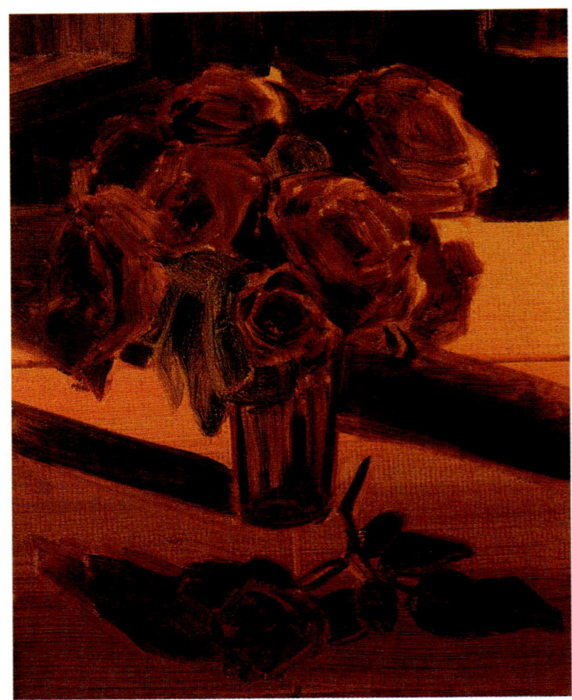

2 When I'm satisfied with the general composition, I begin designating the light, medium, and dark values. With a small flat brush and a thinned mix of alizarin crimson and dioxazine purple, I plot out the dark and light areas on the roses, the crystal vase, and the background. I'm careful to note that the light is coming from the left, and carefully mimic the shadow shapes. Then I begin the dark background with a combination of dioxazine purple, alizarin crimson, and ultramarine blue.

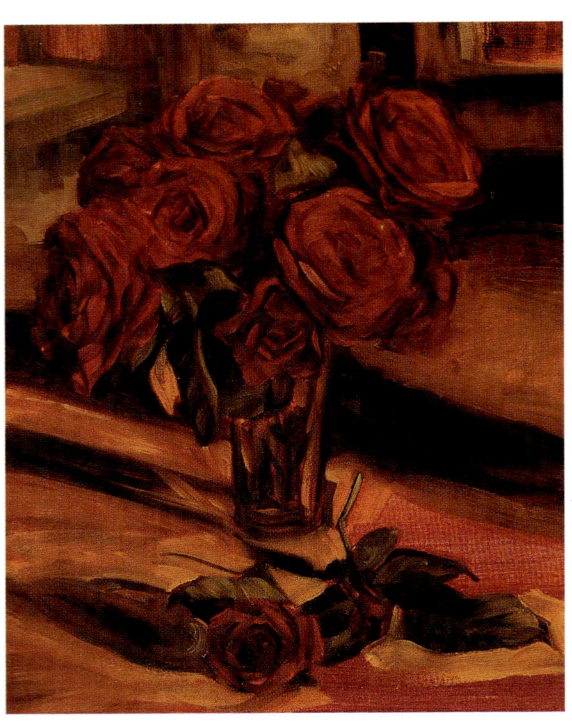

3 Now I use a combination of alizarin crimson, ultramarine blue, and a touch of dioxazine purple to paint the dark shadow and background areas. For the dark values of the roses, I use a small flat brush and a mix of alizarin crimson and magenta. Then, while the paint is still wet, I add the mid-range rose values with alizarin crimson and cadmium red medium. For the dark foliage colors, I use combinations of sap green and alizarin crimson. Next I block in the wooden table with the dark shadow mixture plus some cadmium yellow medium. I use the same color mixture with added titanium white to suggest the wall and window ledges in the background.

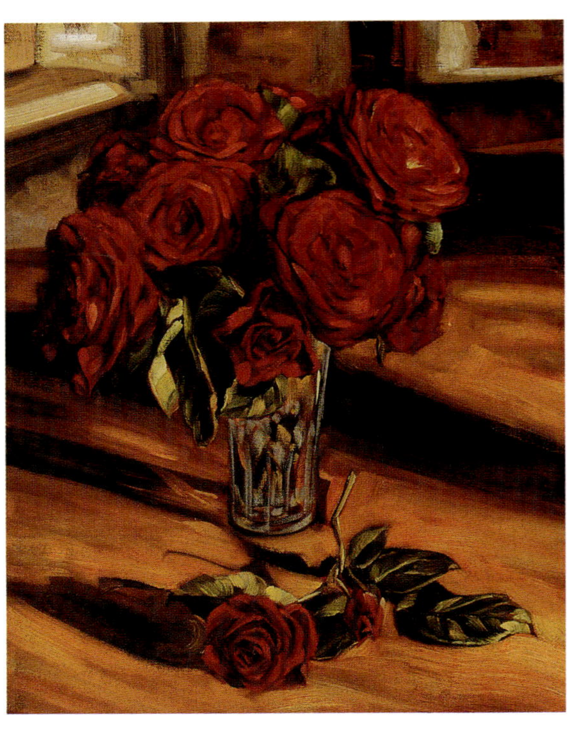

4 Now I layer the medium tones with mixes of alizarin crimson and cadmium red medium in selected parts of all the roses, always keeping the direction of the light source in mind. I also use cadmium red light and permanent rose mixes to create dimension in the flowers. For the medium tones in the leaves, I use sap green and cadmium yellow light. In the vase, I introduce some of the background colors mixed with touches of titanium white. Remember that clear glass has no color of its own, but reflects the colors in the surrounding objects. For the lighter areas of the table, I use a large brush and broad strokes of alizarin crimson, dioxazine purple, and lemon yellow.

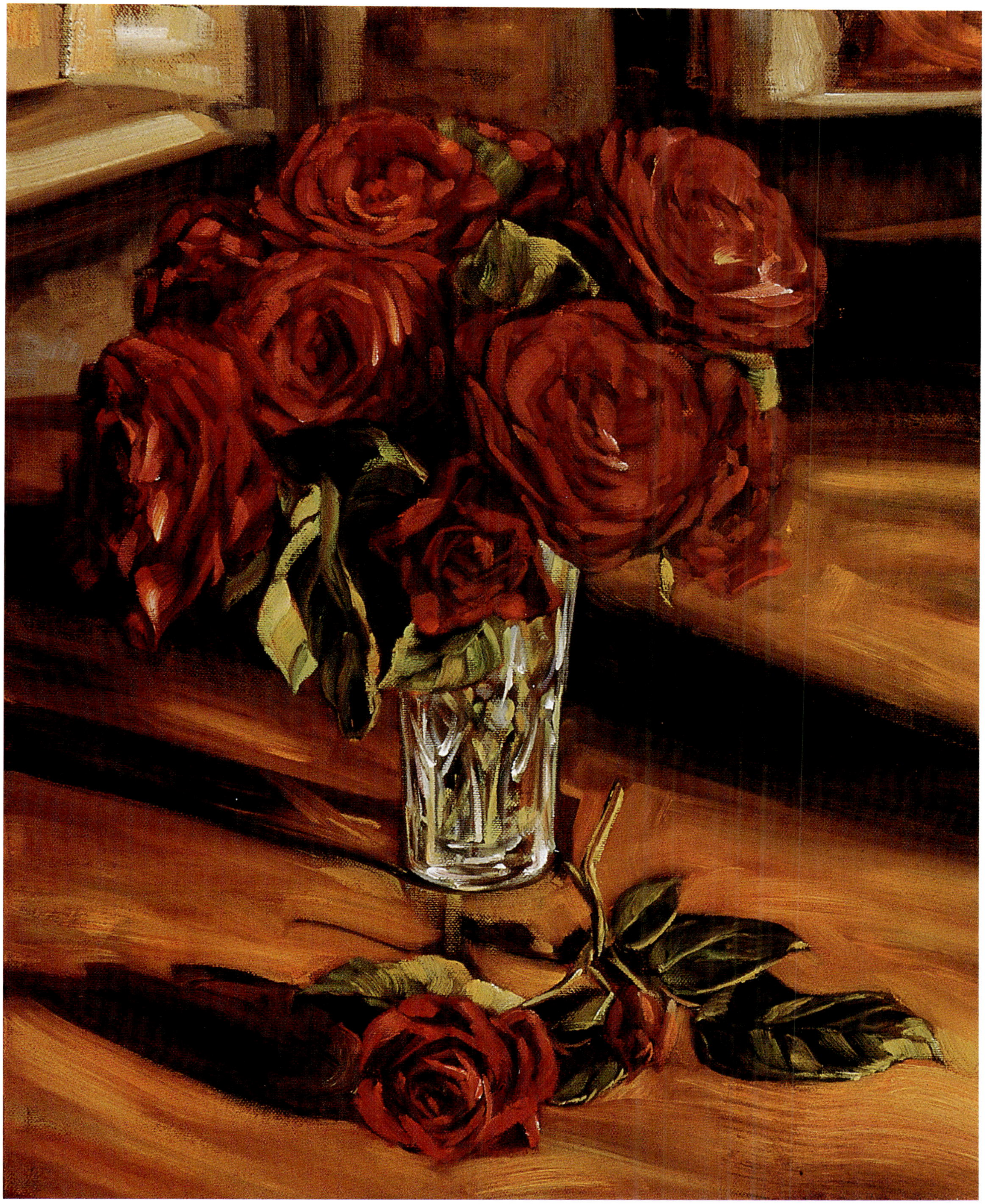

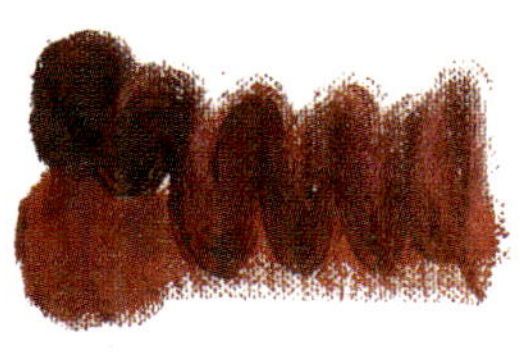

ROSE PETAL DARKS
Alizarin crimson + magenta

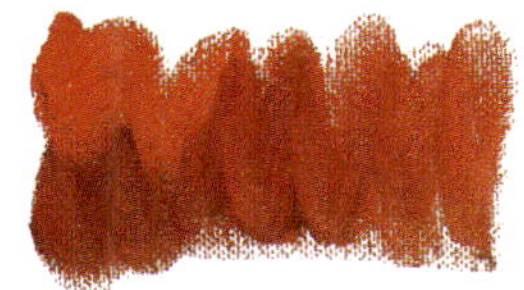

ROSE PETAL MID-RANGE DARKS
Alizarin crimson + cadmium red medium

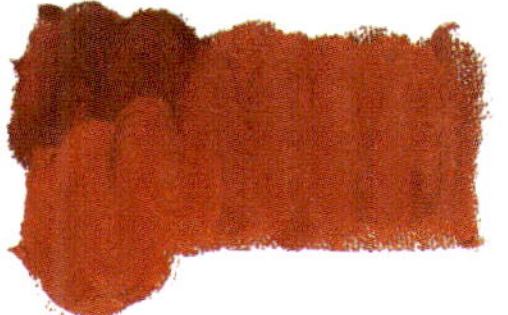

ROSE PETAL MID-RANGE
Cadmium red medium + permanent rose

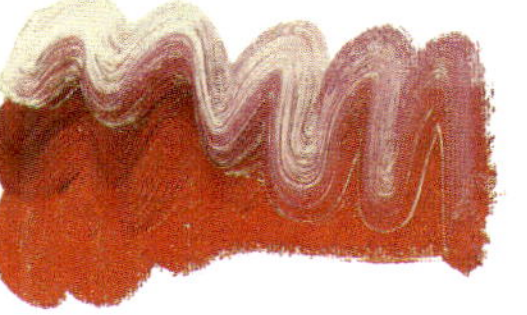

ROSE PETAL HIGHLIGHTS
Cadmium red light + permanent rose + titanium white

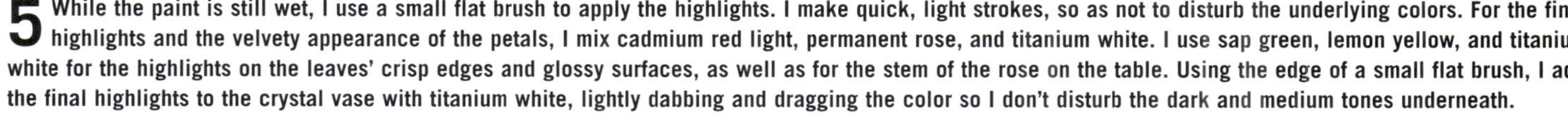

5 While the paint is still wet, I use a small flat brush to apply the highlights. I make quick, light strokes, so as not to disturb the underlying colors. For the final highlights and the velvety appearance of the petals, I mix cadmium red light, permanent rose, and titanium white. I use sap green, lemon yellow, and titanium white for the highlights on the leaves' crisp edges and glossy surfaces, as well as for the stem of the rose on the table. Using the edge of a small flat brush, I add the final highlights to the crystal vase with titanium white, lightly dabbing and dragging the color so I don't disturb the dark and medium tones underneath.

BACKGROUND DARKS
Alizarin crimson + ultramarine blue + dioxazine purple

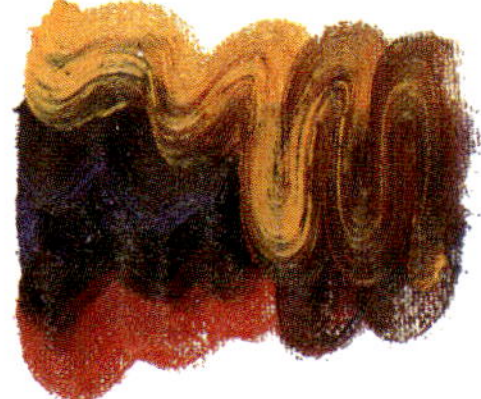

BACKGROUND MID-RANGE
Alizarin crimson + ultramarine blue + dioxazine purple + cadmium yellow medium

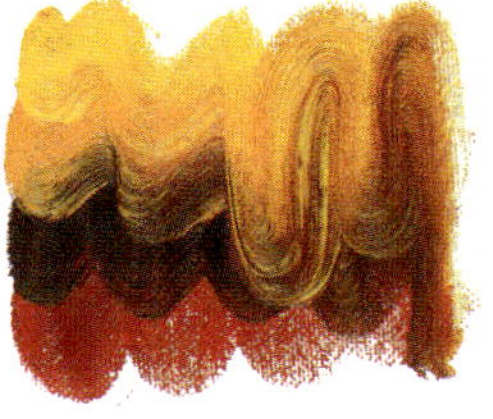

BACKGROUND HIGHLIGHTS
Alizarin crimson + dioxazine purple + cadmium yellow medium + lemon yellow

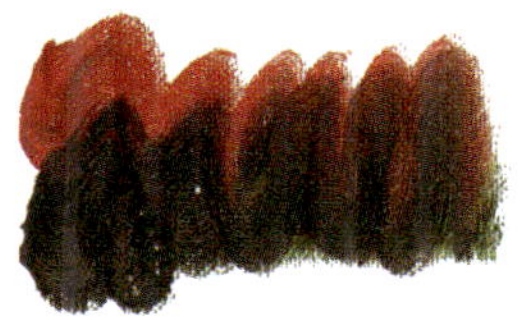

FOLIAGE DARKS
Sap green + alizarin crimson

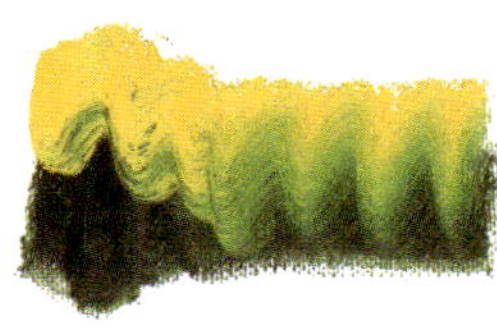

FOLIAGE MID-RANGE
Sap green + cadmium yellow light

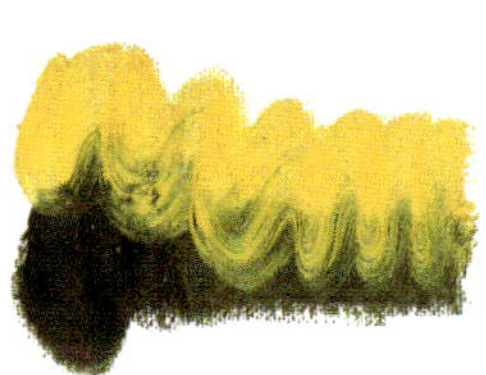

FOLIAGE HIGHLIGHTS
Sap green + lemon yellow

Walter Foster Art Instruction Program

THREE EASY STEPS TO LEARNING ART

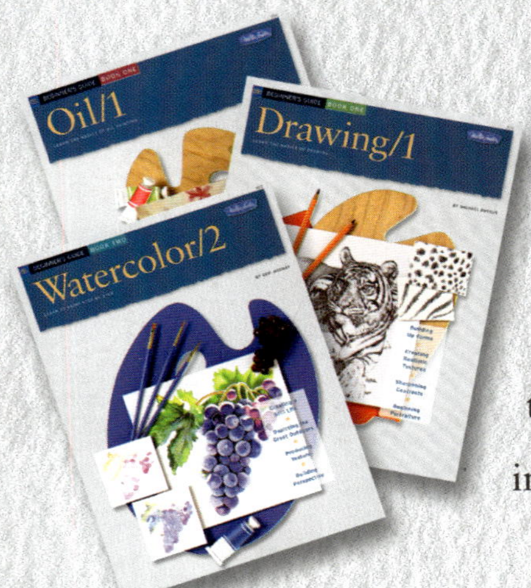

Beginner's Guides are specially written to encourage and motivate aspiring artists. This series introduces the various painting and drawing media—acrylic, oil, pastel, pencil, and watercolor—making it the perfect starting point for beginners. Book One introduces the medium, showing some of its diverse possibilities through beautiful rendered examples and simple explanations, and Book Two instructs with a set of engaging art lessons that follow an easy step-by-step approach.

How to Draw and Paint titles contain progressive visual demonstrations, expert advice, and simple written explanations that assist novice artists through the next stages of learning. In this series, professional artists tap into their experience to walk the reader through the artistic process step by step, from preparation work and preliminary sketches to special techniques and final details. Organized by medium, these books provide insight into an array of subjects.

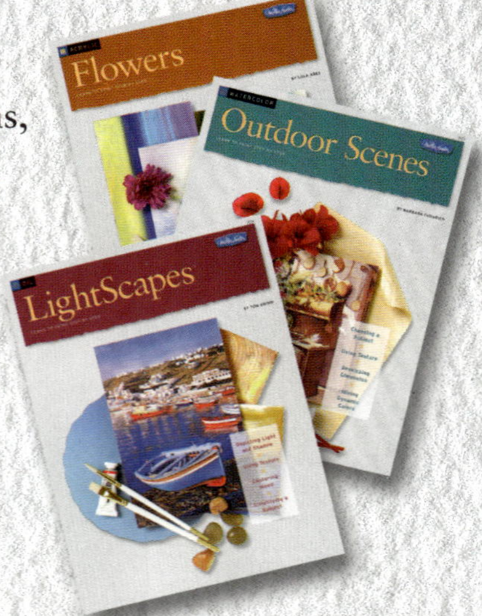

Artist's Library titles offer both beginning and advanced artists the opportunity to expand their creativity, conquer technical obstacles, and explore new media. Written and illustrated by professional artists, the books in this series are ideal for anyone aspiring to reach a new level of expertise. They'll serve as useful tools that artists of all skill levels can refer to again and again.

WALTER FOSTER PUBLISHING, INC.
23062 La Cadena Drive
Laguna Hills, California 92653
Main Line 949/380-7510
Toll Free 800/426-0099

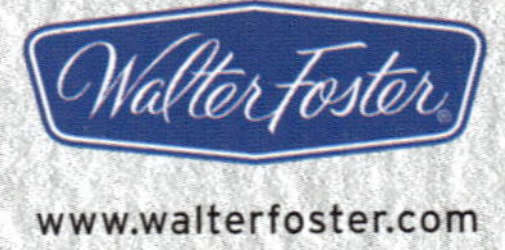

www.walterfoster.com